W9-ASK-999

MATT RAWLE

Author of *The Redemption of Scrooge*

THE GRACE OF
Les Misérables

Abingdon Press/Nashville

The Grace of *Les Misérables*

For Lori, Donna, Nancy, and Kyle,
who taught me the beauty
of music and drama.

CONTENTS

INTRODUCTION

Victor Hugo's *Les Misérables* is a masterpiece. Whether you've been one of the seventy million people in forty-two countries who have experienced the Broadway musical, brave enough to tackle the 1,400-page book that's been translated into twenty-two languages, or you've seen the many movie or television adaptations, you already know the power of this story. Through an abundantly detailed look at early nineteenth-century life in and around Paris, Hugo challenges us to wrestle with the nature of grace, the fault of unwavering justice, the tragedy of poverty, the victory of love, the struggle for justice, and ultimately hope.

Although you might not find *Les Misérables* in the Christian section of your local bookstore or digital reader, Hugo's story is steeped in Christian imagery and ethics. This story is built around the life of the redeemed criminal, Jean Valjean, and his quest to discover the peace of God's grace. His story is not unlike our own. Grace does indeed offer a "peace that surpasses all understanding," but it often takes a lifetime to experience. Like Valjean, we struggle with making holy choices, how to wrestle with poverty and injustice, and how to share love within a world in desperate need of hope.

Les Misérables invites us to see what happens when grace and justice collide. Can mercy and the law exist in the same place at the same time? Are grace and justice mutually exclusive, or might these ideas be one and the same? Hugo also wants the reader to understand that our lives are intimately connected with each other. Our actions are never as independent as we might imagine. One person's decision affects someone else's life, sometimes in grand and dramatic ways. Through politics and love, revolution and forgiveness, *Les Misérables* is a story that continues to capture our imagination!

THE POP IN CULTURE

What comes to mind when you hear someone refer to pop culture? Do you think of movies and colorful characters, or a childhood spent listening to your favorite musicals? These days, we often associate pop culture with television and the characters and personalities we find there, but musicals have dramatically shaped the way we share our story. With the recent advent of musicals like *Hamilton*, and the many live broadcasts of *Rent*, *Peter Pan*, and *Jesus Christ Superstar* on prime-time television, musicals are seeing a resurgence in the popular arena.

Whether or not you enjoy musicals as an art form, there's no denying that popular music, books, television, movies, and media have much to say about the world in which we live. The word *culture* is used often by many different people in many different ways, but in its simplest form, culture is simply an expression of how a community understands itself. God, our Creator, supplies us with the raw ingredients of humanity—talents, time, creativity, desires, ingenuity—and culture is whatever we cook up. Stories,

8

songs, recipes, traditions, art, and language are all displays of how we interpret the world and our place in it.

So what role does God play in our culture—in our day-to-day lives and in the work of our hands, which produce music and art and crafts and literature and plays and movies and technology? Throughout history, people have debated this issue and adamantly drawn a dividing line between that which should be considered *sacred* (that which is explicitly religious in nature) and that which should be considered *secular* (that is, everything else). At first glance, these may be seemingly easy judgments to make, but when we stop to examine what God has to say about this division, we might be surprised at what we find.

Scripture says that all things were made through Christ (John 1:3), and through Christ all things were reconciled to God (Colossians 1:20). In other words, everything and everyone in our world contains a spark of the divine—everything is sacred, and whether or not we choose to live in that truth depends on our perspective. For example, think of sunlight as a holy (sacred) gift from God. God offers us sunlight so we can see the world around us. We can celebrate the sacred by creating things that enhance the light in our homes, such as larger windows or skylights, or we can hang heavy drapes and close the shutters in order to diminish the sacred and shut out the light. Our sacred work is letting in as much light as possible, and those things that keep the light out need to be rejected or transformed. Through Jesus, God put on flesh and walked among us in our world in order to re-narrate what it means to be a child of God.

God assumed culture and transformed it. So now all is sacred, and in everything we are to see and proclaim his glory. I truly believe we are called not to reject the culture we live in, but to re-narrate its meaning—to tell God's story in the midst of it. Jesus didn't reject the cross (the sin of our world); rather, Jesus accepted it and transformed it from a death instrument into a symbol of life and reconciliation.

Sometimes it's easy to see God in the midst of culture—in the stories of Scripture and in reverent hymns and worshipful icons. Stories of heroes and superheroes often preach the gospel pretty clearly, I think. But other times the divine is more veiled—hidden in a novel, concealed in classic rock, obscured by an impressionist's palette. That is why we created this Pop in Culture series, a collection of studies about faith and popular culture. Each study uses a feature of pop culture as a way to examine questions and issues of the Christian faith. Our hope and prayer is that these studies will open our eyes to the spiritual truths that exist all around us in books, movies, music, and television . . . or even musicals.

As we walk with Christ, we discover the divine all around us, and in turn, the world invites us into a deeper picture of its Creator. Through this lens of God's redemption story, we are invited to look at culture in a new and inviting way. We are invited to dive into the realms of literature, art, and entertainment to explore and discover how God is working in and through us and in the world around us to tell God's great story of grace.

A Quick Refresher

Key Characters

- **Jean Valjean**—French peasant who goes to prison for nineteen years for stealing a loaf of bread and finds redemption
- **Javert**—police inspector who disdains all who overstep the bounds of law and who wants Valjean arrested for his crimes
- **Fantine**—young mother of Cosette who is mistreated by society and tragically dies
- **Cosette**—innocent daughter of Fantine who is raised and loved by Valjean and who marries Marius
- **Marius**—young son of Georges Pontmercy who falls in love with Cosette and joins the uprising of 1832

Plot Summary

Les Misérables by Victor Hugo tells the story of the transformation of Jean Valjean from hardened criminal capable of impetuous evil into loving benefactor of a vulnerable child whose mother dies as a result of unjust actions. This historical novel, first published in 1862, is set in France from 1789 to 1833 and focuses on the June 5–6, 1832, uprising in Paris in the aftermath of the French Revolution.

When Jean Valjean is released from a French prison in 1815 after serving nineteen years for stealing a loaf of bread (five-year sentence with fourteen years added for escapes), he is directed to the lowly house of a bishop nicknamed M. Bienvenu ("Welcome"). Valjean is welcomed. He repays the bishop's generosity by stealing silver plates but is arrested and brought back to the scene of the crime. M. Bienvenu tells the police that the plates were a gift and so were the silver candlesticks, which he insists Valjean take as well. Once released, Valjean steals a coin from a boy and regrets it. Although he tries to find the boy, he does not succeed. He weeps.

In 1817, four students in Paris romance four women. After a time of pleasure, the men abandon their mistresses to return to parents and duty. One of the women, Fantine, is pregnant and has a daughter, Cosette. In her poverty, Fantine, 22, asks an innkeeper family, the Thénardiers, to care for her child temporarily. Fantine is on her way to her hometown to try to find work. The Thénardiers do keep Cosette, but, unbeknownst to Fantine, abuse and neglect the child. They greedily demand higher payments from Fantine.

Jean Valjean, toward the end of 1818, has come into Fantine's village, invented a new manufacturing process, and become prosperous. Valjean, who goes by the name Madeleine, uses his profits to help people. He becomes mayor.

Javert, the police inspector, is suspicious of Madeleine and thinks he's seen him somewhere before. Javert witnesses Madeleine saving Father Fauchelevent from being crushed under a cart. This sparks recognition in Javert because he knew of only one man capable of accomplishing such a feat of strength—Jean Valjean, a convict in the galleys. When Fauchelevent recovers, Madeleine obtains a job for him as a gardener at a convent.

Fantine works in Madeleine's factory. She dreams of Cosette. Nosy shop workers discover that Fantine has a child.

At this discovery, the overseer dismisses Fantine without telling Madeleine. Fantine falls into despair, debt, sickness, and prostitution trying to keep up with the incessant demands of the Thénardiers. At her lowest point, Fantine is arrested for attacking a man who was taunting her and sentenced to six months in prison. Madeleine then walks into the station, learns of her dismissal, saves her from Javert's sentencing, and says he'll pay her debts and reunite her with her child.

Madeleine goes to the trial of a man accused of stealing apples and who is mistakenly thought to be Jean Valjean. The mayor proclaims that he, Madeleine, is Valjean. He leaves, expecting arrest.

Valjean sees Fantine, who's very ill, the next day. Javert arrives. The arrest scene and her realization that Cosette isn't there are the death blow for Fantine. Valjean goes to city prison. The next day, he escapes, returns to his house, and packs the silver candlesticks. He barely escapes the clutches of Javert.

The narrator takes a walk in 1861 on the battlefield of Waterloo. He describes the horror and bloodshed at Chateau Hougomont, where Napoleon encountered his first resistance at Waterloo. English, German, and French blood flowed. The narrator reviews the time leading up to and during the epic battle of June 18, 1815.

Robbers went through this battlefield stealing from the fallen. One such man, Thénardier, steals from a motionless French officer. Officer Georges Pontmercy is somehow roused and thanks Thénardier for saving his life.

In 1823, Jean Valjean has been recaptured and is back in the galleys at Toulon for a life sentence. The prosperity of his town disappears. In November 1823, sentenced to labor on a ship, Valjean saves a sailor from falling into the sea; Valjean falls into the sea himself and is presumed dead. He actually survives and reaches Paris.

On Christmas evening 1823, Cosette is eight and still living in misery with the Thénardiers. Cosette is ordered to go to the spring to fetch a bucket of water. Valjean happens to meet her as she trudges. Valjean discovers that she's the daughter of Fantine.

He gives the innkeepers 1,500 francs and leaves with Cosette for Paris. Cosette is happy living with Valjean in an old dwelling called the Gorbeau house. Valjean teaches her to read and to pray and tells her about her mother. Cosette calls him father.

Valjean, who has the appearance of a poor man, gives money to beggars and earns a reputation as the beggar who hands out alms. Javert tracks him down, so Valjean flees with Cosette. They land in the garden of a convent. Fauchelevent works there as a gardener, the job Valjean (as Madeleine) had obtained for him. Fauchelevent recognizes Madeleine and welcomes him and the child into his shanty and gives them refuge. Valjean and Cosette live for several years in the convent, Cosette a happy pupil and Valjean an assistant gardener.

Eight years later the old Gorbeau house is inhabited by the indigent Thénardiers. They now go by the name Jondrette; their young son Gavroche is a street urchin.

Next to the Jondrettes lives a poor young man named Marius Pontmercy. Marius's father is Georges Pontmercy; his grandfather is M. Gillenormand. Huge political differences divide the family and alienate the grandfather, father, and Marius. Gillenormand detests Napoleon. His son-in-law, Pontmercy, fought for Napoleon and was a colonel and a baron. Marius eventually learns the truth about his father's courage, heroism, and honor on the battlefield, including at Waterloo, as well as his father's love for him.

Marius first sees Cosette in the Luxembourg Gardens. He falls in love with her, but they don't speak because she is with an older man. Marius discovers where they live. In May 1832, Marius and Cosette meet every night in her garden. One night Cosette sadly tells Marius that her father said she might need to go away with him soon. Marius quickly asks his grandfather for permission to marry. Gillenormand insults Marius instead, so Marius leaves immediately; the grandfather feels anguish.

Marius despairs over his future with Cosette. His friends—the Friends of the ABC—are preparing to go to the funeral of beloved

General Lamarque. Marius pays little attention and wanders the streets, hearing strange sounds. At the appointed hour he's at the garden, but Cosette isn't there. It's deserted. He feels like dying. A voice says his friends are expecting him in the Rue de la Chanvrerie.

More extraordinary sounds break out; it is the uprising. A band led by Enjolras increases in number as they march. Some of them cry, "To the barricades!" They end up in the Rue Saint Denis.

Friends in the group gather at the Corinthe wine shop, a meeting place for the insurgents on the Rue de la Chanvrerie, on the morning of June 5 and talk of the procession they've seen. Later they hear cries to arms. They are in a good place for a barricade, so they rush into the Rue de la Chanvrerie. The frightened street closes its shops and windows. The fifty barricaders grab whatever they can and build, finishing at twilight. Gavroche names Javert a spy, so Enjolras has him tied up. Marius reaches the Corinthe. That night the barricades are fired upon.

That same evening Valjean learns of a love letter Cosette has written to her dearest. By recalling certain circumstances, Valjean correctly surmises who the young man is but doesn't know his name. He hates the man. Then, by intercepting a love letter from Marius to Cosette, he learns that Marius expects to die and that he is barricaded in the Rue de la Chanvrerie. Valjean heads to the fighting.

At the barricade thirty-seven men are still alive. They realize that the people will not come to support them and that they will be attacked by the whole army of Paris soon. Valjean appears. Marius says he knows him. The fighting does much damage to the Corinthe. Cannons attack the Rue de la Chanvrerie as other barricades are attacked. Enjolras, the leader, orders that Javert be killed by the last man to leave. Valjean volunteers to do it. Once alone with Javert, Valjean frees him unharmed. Javert walks away astonished and annoyed. The army attacks like a hurricane. More Friends of the ABC are killed. Marius is badly wounded. A final assault succeeds.

Valjean carries the unconscious Marius and finds an escape into the sewers of Paris. Valjean doesn't know the way, nearly runs into the police, encounters rats, overcomes mire, and feels his strength failing, but he makes it out, whereupon he sees Javert. Valjean asks Javert to help him take the wounded and still-unconscious man home. Javert's carriage takes them to the house of Gillenormand. Valjean then asks Javert to allow him to go home for an instant. Javert directs the driver to take them. Valjean wants to tell Cosette where Marius is. Javert tells Valjean he will wait for him in the street.

But instead, Javert walks to the Seine. Duty is divided within his conscience. Contrary to all the regulations and the entire code, he has just decided upon a release. It makes Javert shudder. Valjean's generosity toward Javert crushes him. Existence seems tremendously difficult. Javert jumps into the water and drowns.

As Marius recovers, his grandfather's heart softens. Marius tells his grandfather he wants to marry and Gillenormand agrees. Cosette and Marius happily wed February 16, 1833.

Valjean decides to tell Marius the next day about his past as a convict. Marius feels a great horror at the news. Valjean says Cosette was an orphan, she needed him, and he loved her. Marius asks him why he is telling him all this. Valjean says his motive is honesty. Marius gradually estranges Valjean. Heartbroken, Valjean's health fails. He laments that he will die without ever seeing Cosette again.

The same evening Valjean is on his deathbed, Marius learns the truth about Valjean—most important, that Valjean was the man who went to the barricades to save him and who bore him through the sewer. Marius now sees Valjean as a man of rare virtue and tells Cosette that he, Marius, has been monstrously ungrateful.

They rush to Valjean, who has great joy upon seeing Cosette. Marius asks for forgiveness. Valjean bequeaths to Cosette the two silver candlesticks, tells her to forgive the Thénardiers, and says that her mother, Fantine, loved her very much. Telling his children to draw even closer, Jean Valjean dies happy.

1

GRACE WELL RECEIVED: THE STORY OF JEAN VALJEAN

*"Jean Valjean, my brother, you no longer belong to what
is evil but to what is good. I have bought your soul to
save it from black thoughts and the spirit of perdition,
and I give it to God."[1]*

All of the characters in Victor Hugo's *Les Misérables* offer us
a profound picture of how we understand and interact with the
world around us, but none has captured our collective imagination
as much as the redeemed criminal Jean Valjean. From stealing a
loaf of bread to feed his sister's family to becoming an unmarred
and saintly figure by the end of the story, Valjean represents our

own struggle with not only understanding what is good, but having the courage to *do* the good. The popular musical based on Hugo's story suggests that Valjean's conversion from criminal to saint happens in the blink of an eye, and his commitment to following a holy path becomes an almost instinctual action. The original story, however, suggests that choosing the good is a daily and often difficult choice. Much like a recovering addict, Valjean struggles with dampening his personal demons for the sake of making holy choices. If we are honest, our story is similar. Always choosing the good would be easy if the good were obvious. Jean Valjean's journey helps us recognize how difficult accepting grace can be, and how sharing grace can sometimes be even more difficult.

The Lenten season invites us into this struggle. The forty days of Lent is time set apart for we who are the body of Christ to give up distractions or adopt spiritual practices that prepare us to celebrate Jesus' resurrection well. Lent is the church's gift to itself. It is neither mentioned nor mandated in the Gospels, but we know ourselves well. As we will discover with Valjean, accepting grace can be difficult work. Sometimes we feel that grace is absurd when it is offered to us. Maybe more often than we care to admit, grace seems wasteful when it's offered to those we don't think deserve it. Other times our faults and failures are so distracting that we don't recognize grace when it is offered. This great season prepares our soul to have the humble vision to recognize that the empty tomb means death is no longer the end of our story. Valjean's story is a helpful way to begin the season. Transformation takes time. Even though Jesus was raised after three days, for us the journey takes much longer.

AN OFFERING OF GRACE

I fell in love with the musical *Les Misérables* when I was in high school. It had everything I was looking for: a hero who was transformed from sinner to saint, romance between two star-crossed lovers, war anthems and revolution, a lot of high notes I could practice singing, and maybe most importantly, the celebration of God's grace. I had seen *Godspell, Jesus Christ Superstar,* and *Joseph and the Amazing Technicolor Dreamcoat,* but none of these musicals seemed real or honest about faith. They all have their place, but *Les Misérables* offers something different.

Les Misérables is a story that wrestles with the intersection between offering grace and maintaining justice. This story doesn't shy away from the devastation of abject poverty and whether armed resistance against those with power is the most appropriate remedy to changing the world. It's the kind of story that leaves you asking better questions about God, the world, and our role within it, rather than offering a nice and polite moral with a curtain call. I could tell they were offering the story of what it means to follow Christ without being labeled as a "Christian" musical. It's one thing to talk about grace, forgiveness, and our role of being in ministry with the poor, but how does this translate to our neighbors when we aren't sitting in a pew or worship center chair? At least for me, this was the kind of story I desperately needed at that time in my Christian walk. When I was young, Christianity seemed like a set of rules to make sure we were polite and that God liked us. The music we sang was sweet, catchy, and always had a moral. There's nothing necessarily wrong with a sweet and easy-to-memorize Bible school song, but the *Les Misérables* musical offered an authenticity that I felt was missing.

Appropriately, this whole story begins with the kindness of a priest, which originates long before we see the criminals singing

19

in the musical's prologue. Monseigneur Myriel was a parish priest in the early nineteenth century in the town of Digne, France. His kindness and selflessness earned him the nickname M. Bienvenu. He was a champion of the poor, often giving money away as quickly as he acquired it. He is a bit of a Robin Hood of sorts, never letting a bit of larceny get in the way of offering money to the poor and destitute, which immediately sets up the ethical tension of whether the end justifies the means. M. Bienvenu always has the end in mind.

Have you ever been in a situation where there is tension between the means and the end, or doing something that might stretch the rules to the point of breaking, but goodness was the end result? Jesus was known to bend the rules for the glory of God. Early in Mark's Gospel, Jesus and the disciples were picking grain on the Sabbath, which was forbidden according to Exodus 34:21—"You should do your work for six days, but on the seventh day you should rest. Even during plowing or harvesttime you should rest" (CEB). The Pharisees were quick to remind Jesus that what they were doing was not permitted, but Jesus replied:

> *"Haven't you ever read what David did when he was in need, when he and those with him were hungry? During the time when Abiathar was high priest, David went into God's house and ate the bread of the presence, which only the priests were allowed to eat. He also gave bread to those who were with him."* . . . *"The Sabbath was created for humans; humans weren't created for the Sabbath."*
> (Mark 2:25-27 CEB)

Sometimes we forget that we are reading this story thousands of years after the Resurrection, knowing that Jesus was the fully human and fully divine Messiah and therefore Jesus has full authority to re-narrate our understanding of God's Law. At the time, the Pharisees had a point. From their point of view, breaking the Law was a sign that you did not trust that God would provide. God allowed a double portion of manna from heaven so that the ancient Israelites would not need to gather on the seventh day. The Pharisees might question the disciples as to why they were hungry. Why did they not gather enough the day before, and do they not trust that God will supply their every need? Jesus' teaching here is less about what to do and what not to do on the Sabbath; rather Jesus is teaching the Pharisees that our commitment to loving our neighbor is the center of God's Law. When there seems to be tension between loving our neighbor and a stipulation of the Law, loving our neighbor wins.

Bending or breaking the rules to meet the needs of others is where Jean Valjean enters the story. Valjean is arrested for stealing bread in order to feed his widowed sister's family. Is it wrong to steal bread in order to feed a starving family? Maybe a better question is why are those who have bread unwilling to share it? Maybe this particular bread maker was finding it difficult to make ends meet, and he wasn't in a place to offer bread at no cost? Maybe an even better question is why a widowed mother is starving in a place so steeped in Christianity as France?

Regardless, Valjean is arrested and given a five-year sentence of hard labor. His various attempts at escape lengthened his sentence to nineteen years. This extended time in the cruel French penal system changed this relatively good and moral man into someone who had become hardened, hopeless, and desperate. After his release he searches for lodging, and even though he has money to offer, he is seen as dangerous and a threat. There was no room for him in the inn, so to speak. After being run off by a dog for resting in a dog house, he finds himself at rock bottom. He says to himself, "I am not even a dog."[2] Even Lazarus didn't scare away the dogs that took to licking his wounds.

He finds himself at the doorstep of M. Bienvenu who, much to Valjean's surprise, welcomes him and offers him supper and a bed for the evening. This welcome Valjean receives reminds me of Jesus' parable about the prodigal son. In essence, the priest puts a ring on his finger, offers him sandals for his feet, and kills the fatted calf for someone seemingly undeserving. Unfortunately, Valjean's reaction to this grace is to steal silver from the priest and make a quick getaway in the middle of the night.

Have you ever offered grace expecting to receive grace in return? I wish I could tell you that grace is always reciprocated, but that wouldn't be the truth. Jesus even reminds us not to offer grace with the expectation of receiving grace in return.

> *"If you love those who love you, why should you be commended? Even sinners love those who love them. If you do good to those who do good to you, why should you be commended? Even sinners do that. If you lend to those from whom you expect repayment, why should you be commended? Even sinners lend to sinners expecting to be paid back in full. Instead, love your enemies, do good, and lend expecting nothing in return. If you do, you will have a great reward. You will be acting the way children of the Most High act, for he is kind to ungrateful and wicked people. Be compassionate just as your Father is compassionate."*
> *(Luke 6:32-36 CEB)*

Lent is a time for us to lean into areas of our walk with Christ that need some attention. Learning to offer grace with no expectation of receiving grace in return is certainly something on which we all can focus as we consider Christ's journey to the cross. For Valjean, offering grace is not yet part of his story. He first must dive into the difficult work of receiving grace, and the art of receiving grace is something that follows him for the rest of his remarkable, redemptive story.

A CHANGED LIFE?

Have you ever had someone tell you that you remind them of someone else? "You remind me of my brother," or "You remind me of my friend growing up." I'm never quite sure how to respond, though I usually end up saying something unremarkable like, "Oh, he must be a funny guy," to which they usually respond, "Not really, but he is bald." Have you ever spent time considering the difference between how we see ourselves and how others see us? Sometimes these pictures can be similar, and other times we are left scratching our heads wondering how someone could see us in a particular way.

After a speaking engagement a few years ago, someone from the audience approached me and said, "You must be a three." I had no idea what she was talking about, so I answered saying, "If that's on a scale from one to ten, you're probably right." She was talking about Enneagram types, a tool used to understand your personal motivations and aversions. On the way home I began researching Enneagram types (and later attended a workshop) and discovered that I am very much not a three. I was left wondering why someone would see me so differently than I see myself. Was I trying to hide who I really was? When I'm in front of a crowd am I pretending to be someone I'm not? Could it be that she was just a poor judge of character? Whatever the case, are we who we think we are? For those well-versed in the Enneagram, you will recognize that asking these questions reveals that I am a solid seven.

The local police apprehend Valjean for stealing the priest's silver in the middle of the night, and when M. Bienvenu is invited to identify Valjean as the thief, the priest surprises everyone. He offers Valjean additional silver, claiming that what Valjean had taken was a gift. After Valjean is released, M. Bienvenu tells Valjean that he must use this silver to become an honest man. This act of kindness is almost too much for Valjean to bear. This is a convicting moment for Valjean. Since his imprisonment he had been incapable of believing that there was good in the world. Not only does the priest reveal that grace exists and can personally be experienced, he offers the challenge and charge to go and do likewise. The message is not to "go and sin no more," as is often lifted up in moments of grace; rather it is a proactive calling to do good.

Following Christ is more than avoiding sin or evading things that distract us from loving God and loving our neighbor. We miss the gospel when we only live a "thou shall not" life. Of course, resisting temptation and recognizing the power of saying "no" is important, but if this is our only goal, we might find ourselves walking on the other side of the road to protect our own purity rather than joining the good Samaritan to care for the man who fell into the hands of robbers (Luke 10).

To say that this moment in the story is Valjean's conversion is not altogether accurate. The kindness M. Bienvenu offers is a conviction unlike this convict had ever received. Valjean's assumption that the world is depraved, without hope of grace, is tried and found to be false. His belief that he is only capable of being a thief is radically turned on its head. His resignation of being "less than a dog" is seemingly excised under the power of this priest's charge. To say that this is Valjean's conversion, a "once and for all" kind of moment, is to deny his struggle that we will see later in the story; but we can certainly say that what he considered to be true about the world, his identity, and his self-worth is a conviction that will soon transform the lives of many.

What do you consider to be true about the world? I remember I was in high school when I first started reading Scripture for myself. It was Holy Week, the week before Easter, when I read Jesus' passion story in the Gospel of Mark in my bedroom before going to bed one night. The high priest, named Caiaphas in other Gospels, asks Jesus if he is the Messiah. Jesus replies, "I am" (Mark 14:62). This answer seems pretty simple and straightforward. I decided to read the same story from Matthew's Gospel to see how they might be different. In Matthew, Caiaphas asks Jesus the same question, but Jesus' answer is different—You say so, but I tell you . . . .

"I am" is not the same as "You say so." I checked Luke and John, and to my astonishment, Jesus' answers were slightly different in each account (and very different in John's Gospel). This Jesus that I had been hearing about from my friends and my church was now both foreign and oddly exciting to me. It's one thing for the Gospels to offer a slightly different picture of what Jesus did and said, but when Jesus' answer to the same simple question is so different, it left me wondering what else I had been missing. This started me on the path to read almost anything I could get my hands on that had anything to do with Scripture. Ultimately this is part of my story in becoming a pastor. Sharing the complexity, beauty, and nuance of Scripture is an opportunity for which I am thankful every day.

During that time in my life, I experienced a great conviction, but conversion had only just begun. The same is true for Valjean. The grace he receives from M. Bienvenu is a great conviction that challenges his worldly assumptions. The priest had every right to hand Valjean over to the police, but he didn't. Instead, he offered him a gift and sent him on his way. Valjean's conviction is powerful, and his conversion is only just beginning.

We sometimes talk about having a "Damascus Road" experience, like the apostle Paul, as if this moment of blinding light, revelation, or new learning causes us to be born again through faith; but Paul was not converted on the road to Damascus. Paul was convicted on the road to Damascus. His assumptions were questioned, his actions called into question, and everything he thought he knew about God seemed to turn upside down. The risen Lord who appeared before Paul had every opportunity to enact a blind justice against Paul. At the very least, Paul approved of the stoning of Stephen. Christ could have asked for Paul's life in that moment. An eye for an eye, so to speak. But this is not the gospel. Paul was convicted on the road to Damascus, but his conversion began when his enemy, a Christian named Ananias, laid hands upon him and healed him. Valjean has now been convicted, but his conversion has just begun. This radical shift he is experiencing is his understanding that he is no longer a convict running from the law; rather he is convict of grace.

Can you put your finger on a time when your assumptions about the world changed? Maybe it was when you had your first child, and you suddenly realized you were no longer living only for yourself. Maybe you came face to face with someone who had the right to treat you just as poorly as you treated that person, but he or she refrained. Maybe you opened the Bible late one night, and everything you thought you knew about Jesus was turned on its head. Conviction changes our perception of the world around us. We are the same, but our perception is different. Conversion is when we, ourselves, begin to change. We discover a holy dance when we live into the graceful conviction of Christ. Our assumptions are challenged, and we move with the Holy Spirit into a new way of life. Then, quite unexpectedly, the Spirit convicts us again, and points us in yet another direction. God is alive, moving, and dynamic, which means that the dance between conviction and conversion is a beautiful and never-ending adventure with the divine.

DISCIPLINE AND RESPONSIBILITY

One of my favorite Scriptures is the beginning of the Book of Acts (1:6-11). Jesus is ascending, promising the power of the Holy Spirit will be offered the disciples, and these Jesus followers are left staring at the sky. Then two men in white robes appear asking them why they were staring into the heavens. It's a great question to an honest reaction. I imagine they were staring into the sky because facing each other was too difficult. "What now?" is a question I'm sure they were thinking. The disciples had seen miracles, heard teachings about the coming Kingdom; they fled when Jesus was arrested, privately mourned Jesus' death, and saw the resurrected Lord in the middle of their shared living room. Then Jesus ascended without giving them a plan other than the promise of receiving the Holy Spirit when they get to Jerusalem. Where do they go from here?

Jean Valjean experienced a life-altering conviction of grace, but he did not receive any kind of blueprint or twelve-step plan as to what he was now supposed to do. He had to improvise. Improvisation is exciting to me, but there also is great comfort in having a road map for what lies ahead. I will confess that my office is full of leadership books on church growth, financial stewardship, and "how tos" of ministry. These tools are certainly helpful, but it is impossible to anticipate everything. So, Valjean does what many of us are tempted to do when life turns upside down. He retreats.

After Jesus was baptized, he fled to the wilderness for forty days. The forty days of the Lenten season are written into our shared liturgical life as a means of both remembering God's story and acting upon it. We remember Noah's forty rainy days and nights sailing on an endless ocean that washed away everything he knew. We remember the ancient Israelites' forty years in the wilderness as they walked together with God to discover what it means to leave the bondage of Egypt to be bound together as God's chosen people. After Jesus hears, "This is my Son, the Beloved, with whom I am well pleased" (Matthew 3:17), he retreats.

This time of retreat isn't escapism; rather it is a time of discernment, preparation, and planning. I suppose Jesus could have moved directly to the cross, but without the context of Jesus' teachings, healings, and miracles, the cross would make even less sense than it does to us today. It's humbling to remember that the whole of Jesus' ministry took three years. With such a brief timeline, Jesus' movement must have been meticulously planned. These forty days in the wilderness were more than prayer and fasting. I imagine Jesus thought deeply about the "what now" question after hearing God's voice coming from the clouds. Whether or not Jesus knew that his earthly ministry would be no more than three years, he surely understood that time was precious. When there isn't much time, you must work slowly, so to speak.[3] Taking time to think, pray, fast, and discern is what the forty days of Lent are about. If we move too quickly to the cross, its offense overshadows its glory. If we wait too long, we find ourselves escaping the embarrassment of God's love on vulnerable display. So, we retreat without escaping, let go without giving up, and work slowly because time is precious.

Jean Valjean doesn't disappear for long. He reenters the story as a successful factory owner and Mayor of Montreuil under the assumed name of M. Madeleine. He is generous and compassionate with worker and citizen alike. One day Valjean noticed a man named Fauchelevent was trapped under his own cart. Although Fauchelevent was known to be a curmudgeon, Valjean quickly lifted the cart and saved his life. One might think that such an act of selflessness and compassion would be well received, but this only raises suspicion from Police Chief Javert that M. Madeleine is none other than the escaped convict, Jean Valjean.

It seems that no good deed goes unpunished (but *Wicked* is a whole other musical). Have you ever been in a situation where doing the right thing led to a difficult outcome? Have you ever thought to yourself that if you choose not to blow a whistle, life would be much more simple? The priest and the Levite were probably thinking the same thing in Jesus' good Samaritan parable

(Luke 10:25-37). A man fell among robbers on the road to Jericho, and they left him half dead. A priest and a Levite walk by on the other side of the road. Scripture doesn't tell us why they chose not to help. It could be that they wanted to abstain from touching the man in order to remain ritually clean. Maybe they were headed to a church meeting that they could not miss. Maybe they thought that being involved would be more trouble than it was worth.

Jesus doesn't seem to care why they walked by on the other side of the road. I assume Jesus is equally concerned with our excuses. Like the "good" Samaritan, Jean Valjean chooses to offer aid with seemingly no regard of the consequences, but he certainly pays quite a price. Javert investigates Valjean's past and becomes convinced that M. Madeleine is the convict's pseudonym. Just before apprehending M. Madeleine, another man fitting Valjean's description is arrested. Javert meets with M. Madeleine to apologize for thinking he was such a crooked person and says that he will be leaving soon to testify that they have, indeed, captured Valjean.

This places Valjean in an ethical dilemma. Does he keep his secret for the good of the life he has built, or does he reveal himself for the good of his own soul? This is not an unfamiliar quandary. Jesus tells the disciples, "Those who love their life lose it, and those who hate their life in this world will keep it for eternal life. Whoever serves me must follow me, and where I am, there will my servant be also. Whoever serves me, the Father will honor" (John 12:25-26). In this context, Valjean isn't worried about life or death; rather he is contemplating what it really means to be alive. Dying for what you believe is arguably easier than living for what you believe. Living as a follower of Jesus is something we are called to do every day and over and over again. Jesus tells the disciples, "If any want to become my followers, let them deny themselves and take up their cross daily and follow me" (Luke 9:23). In other words, carrying the cross isn't a one-time obligation.

29

Valjean has a sleepless night, full of vivid and terrifying dreams. After seeing a vision of M. Bienvenu, Valjean finally decides to get his affairs in order and give himself up. The next morning he races to the courthouse in Arras, but his agony is not finished. His carriage wheel is broken during the journey, so he tries to rent another carriage or find another horse. Nothing is available. He resigns to himself that he tried to do the right thing, but it doesn't seem to be working out. Who can blame Valjean for interpreting his difficulty as a sign that he is making the wrong decision?

It's funny how we interpret the signs that we think we see. Discerning God's will through signs can be a tricky affair. If we're being honest, we tend to look for signs that affirm our decisions, rather than deepening our relationship with God, which can make our decisions more clear to begin with. As James Howell puts it, "A hunch about God's will might by sheer luck coincide with God's will, but can't we . . . admit we look for signs that work to our benefit and ignore any that might demand serious sacrifice? Should we rely on quirky spiritual happenstances, or instead rely on our closeness to God?"[4] Eventually, Valjean does make his way to the courtroom and confesses his true identity. To his amazement he is allowed to freely leave the courtroom and return home, but Javert is quick to follow.

At this point it is important to mention Fantine, a character we will discuss more in chapter 3. Fantine is a young woman who was working in Valjean/M. Madeleine's factory. A superintendent dismisses her from her position, and she falls deep into poverty while trying to pay an innkeeper who is extorting her for caring for her daughter, Cosette. When Valjean returns to find Fantine on her deathbed, he feels great remorse and responsibility for her state. He promises to find her child and care for her as her own, but Javert, who followed him from the courthouse quickly arrests him. Later that evening, Valjean escapes from prison, gathers his belongings, and sets out to find Cosette and once again assume a new identity.

We begin to see that Valjean's desire to lead a moral life isn't easy. First, there's the difficulty in understanding what the good is—remain hidden for the sake of others, or confess for the sake of his own soul? Second, following through with doing good is easier said than done. Although he had a powerful convicting experience, discerning and executing the good is a daily struggle. It's a daily struggle for us as well. Is this meeting more important than my son's baseball game? Should I speak up when I see something unfair in the workplace? Will the IRS really know if I fudge some numbers? I imagine that Jesus' words, "Nothing is hidden that won't be revealed, and nothing is secret that won't be brought out into the open" (Luke 12:2 CEB), are a great motivator for Valjean. It is often the case that Jesus' words offer both challenge and justice. Knowing that "whatever you have whispered in the rooms deep inside the house will be announced from the rooftops" (Luke 12:3 CEB) should give us great pause when we are tempted to gossip, tell a half-truth, or say something we shouldn't. On the other hand, if you've ever been harmed, defeated, or slighted by whispers spoken out of the corner of mouths, this is a verse over which to give thanks. For Valjean, knowing that all things will be revealed propels him into doing good, but he isn't quite ready for all of his secrets to be known.

A SALVATION OF SECRETS

In high school I spent a lot of time in practice. Whether it was on the field with football, in my room with homework, or rehearsing what I would say to the young woman whom I hoped would go to the dance with me, practice is what I did with most of my time. In particular I spent most of my time at play practice. I loved being in

31

plays and musicals for many reasons, but what I appreciated about them the most is that being on stage gave me an excuse to study what it would be like to be someone else. For a short time I could pretend that I was the suave gangster, Sky Masterson, from *Guys and Dolls*, or the heroic romantic Ralph Rackstraw in *H.M.S. Pinafore*.

With each role the director would often ask, "What is your character's motivation?" What desires are they trying to fulfill? Why do they do what they do? It's one thing to show up at your mark at the precise time and say your lines perfectly, but when an actor doesn't quite understand who the character is, the performance seems inauthentic. I've been told that the character's motivation is what happens between the dialogue. Motivation is unspoken, but it "says" the most.

What motivates you? Maybe it depends on your goal. Your goal may be to lose ten pounds, but the motivation is fitting into the clothes you bought last year that you want to wear again. Your goal might be to make a good grade on the final exam, but the motivation is learning new skills, or at least making a better grade than the other guy. Your goal is the end point, but motivation is what drives you to reach for your goal. So, which is more important? A goal seems impossible without the drive to accomplish it. It's also difficult to maintain passion without a goal to reach. So, is the "what" (goal) or the "why" (motivation) more important in our daily walk?

When Valjean decides to raise Cosette as his own, the goal of keeping his vow seems to be the only thing on his mind. Initially, it doesn't seem to matter whether his goal is moral, right, or correct. It's a promise he's made, and he will do whatever he needs to in order to fulfill it. With only a goal in mind, there's little room for discussion on whether the end justifies the means. Valjean collects Cosette from Thénardier and his wife, who manage a less than reputable inn. After negotiating a price to relieve them of

Cosette, which is best described as a tolerable extortion, Valjean and Cosette head off to Paris to assume new identities with a quiet life. Their unassuming presence begins to raise suspicion in the community, and Javert begins to investigate. When Valjean recognizes that Javert is close, he and Cosette quickly leave yet again to assume a new identity in a new place.

After wandering in the bitter cold, Cosette is close to death. Valjean calls out to a man walking in a garden to plead that he might take them in. To his utter astonishment, the man calls out to Valjean, recognizing him as M. Madeleine. The man in the garden is Fauchelevent, the man Valjean saved from a cart accident earlier in the story. He takes them in and keeps Valjean's identity a secret. For the first time Valjean is beginning to see a glimmer of reward for the decisions he's made. More to the point, this is the first time we see Valjean's redemption taking root. He's beginning to recognize that goodness is not simply a promise to be kept in order to repay M. Bienvenu for his kindness, but goodness is a reward in and of itself. In other words, for the first time Valjean begins to experience a motivation for good. Goodness no longer is an obligation but a desire. We begin to see a "why" to his "what."

Lent is a time when we dive into the relationship between the "what" and the "why" of our faith. For example, often we give something up or take something on for Lent. Sometimes we give up food that we particularly love or we make a commitment to a new prayer routine. Lenten disciplines often are framed as commitments to obedience. We fast, pray, deny, and fulfill through a joyful obedience as a child of God. Obedience may seem to be the goal, but this isn't the gospel. The goal of spiritual disciplines during Lent isn't to craft a keen sense of obedience, even though obedience is important. The point is transformation. It's one thing to serve on a mission trip out of a sense of obedience. It is quite another to fall in love with serving itself.

Last summer I had the great fortune to attend two very different weddings. At the first, the pastor lifted up the importance of obedience within the wedding vows, emphasizing that through obedience to Christ, husband and wife love one another in a covenantal relationship. At the second wedding, the pastor emphasized that because the bride and groom love each other, they will live in obedience within the vows of their marriage. So, does one come before the other? Do we love because we are obedient, or are we obedient because we love? They certainly aren't mutually exclusive. In Micah we hear, "He has told you, O mortal what is good, / What does the LORD require of you? / but to do justice, and to love kindness, / and to walk humbly with your God" (6:8). To love and to walk go hand in hand, but which do we experience first? For Valjean his obedience to the promise he made to Fantine leads him to loving Cosette as his own.

Obedience is a fine place to start. In the case of Lenten disciplines, we see how obedience can lead to love—like a runner who makes a commitment to run every morning and eventually can't not run at dawn, or the young dancer who begrudgingly attends ballet class and years later can't imagine doing anything else. The things we give up and take on are meant to lead us into a transformative love. You may pick up a new routine of praying first thing in the morning for the forty days of Lent, and the hope is that you fall in love with going to God when your eyes first open in the morning. It's like when John Wesley was having a crisis of faith. He met with his friend Peter Bohler, who offered interesting advice. "Preach faith till you have it; and then, because you have it, you will preach faith."[5] But obedience isn't the goal. It's like when Jesus healed a man on the Sabbath. When the Pharisees presented Jesus with a man with a withered hand, they watched him closely to see what he would do. Jesus first asked them a question—"Which is lawful on the Sabbath: to do good or to do evil, to save life or to kill?" (Mark 3:4 NIV). Jesus wasn't being obedient to the letter of the law, but through love Christ revealed obedience to God. Love motivated obedience.

Valjean is beginning to love, which informs his actions for the rest of the story. Since his interaction with M. Bienvenu, commitment, keeping promises, and personal morality are his motivations for repaying the kindness of the priest he met so many years ago. Things are changing. Now love is becoming the motivation, and interestingly love is also becoming the goal. In other words, what Valjean is beginning to discover is that love is both motivation and the goal itself.

CONFESSION AND HONESTY

Do you know someone who is either a proverbial "early bird" or a "night owl"? I have always been an early bird. Even during my teenage years it was rare for me to sleep past 7:00 a.m. The fact that I wake up early and my wife naturally stays up late became very useful when we started having kids. Since our first child never seemed to sleep (at all), my wife and I came to an agreement. She would take the late shift (10:00 p.m.–2:00 a.m.), and I would take the early shift (3:00 a.m.–7:00 a.m.). If our daughter woke up during the "witching hour" between 2:00 and 3:00 a.m., my wife and I would play a game that I consider to be a version of freeze tag where we would both try to remain as still as possible to pretend that neither of us heard the monitor in the hope that the other person would get out of bed.

Getting through the sleep deprivation of that first year of being new parents was difficult, but we made it through. Interestingly there was an unintended consequence that I hadn't considered. Even after our daughter started sleeping through the night, I found myself naturally waking up around 3:00 a.m. I've heard it said that it takes about sixty-six days for a new habit to take root, so after about 300 days of waking up at 3:00 a.m., it seems this new habit was hopelessly ingrained as a new behavior.

Have you experienced unintended consequences within your Christian walk? Even though the Lenten season falls short of the sixty-six day threshold for new habits, giving something up or taking on something for Lent is to be transformational. It makes little sense to stop your new prayer routine or start eating more chocolate than you should once Easter has rolled around. In a way, the forty days of Lent is a glimpse of sanctifying grace—the power of the Holy Spirit that transforms who we are and conforms us into the image of Christ.

Near the end of *Les Misérables*, Valjean begins to experience this sanctifying grace of the Holy Spirit after a lifetime of struggling to actively choose the good. Although there is more to Valjean's story that we will cover in other chapters, there are two moments that represent his ultimate victory. Marius, a young man in love with Cosette whom we will discuss later, is injured during an insurgent uprising against the government. Valjean sees Marius as a threat to his own happiness because of his pursuing Cosette, the one person Valjean has grown to love. Initially Valjean considers leaving him to die, which would allow Valjean to continue to live happily in secret with his daughter. Choosing the good has never been an instinctive venture for Valjean. His actions have always been a daily weighing of ethical implications. He eventually decides to save Marius's life for the sake of his daughter, dragging Marius through the Paris sewers to reach safety.

The sewers represent a sort of Hell for Valjean. There's very little light to illuminate the labyrinth of pathways. He's carrying Marius over one shoulder and feeling the walls with his other. You get the sense that Valjean carrying Marius is like Jesus carrying the cross. He is continually descending into darkness for the sake of someone else's life. Eventually the pavement under his feet gives way, and he has to trudge through waste in which it is deep enough to drown. This, in a way, was his final descent. He feels pavement again and is consumed with a new energy to push forward and find a way out.

We may not have had to drag a dying man through the Paris sewers, but we have all experienced some kind of darkness in our journey. Maybe you've experienced the death of someone you treasured, or your health declined and left you questioning your value. Maybe you've heard the words, "I don't love you," or "We're going to have to let you go." I've heard folks dismiss the difficulty in his or her life by saying that others certainly must have it worse. Although that may be true, with darkness there is little gradation. Sometimes life seems pitch black, and other times all it takes is for weeping to close our eyes. Either way, in that moment it seems that there is little light. Christ's death and resurrection teach us that darkness, though present and real, will never have the final word. Valjean made it out of the sewer, Jesus' tomb was empty, and we too will one day experience resurrection.

But the story isn't finished. Is it ever? Marius regains his strength and plans to wed Cosette. It almost seems too good to be true, and unfortunately it is. In order for Marius and Cosette to be married, Valjean would have to finally confess who he is, because signing the papers for their marriage under a pseudonym would risk the validity of their marriage. So Valjean has a convenient accident that leaves him unable to sign the marriage documents; Marius's grandfather, M. Gillenormand, performs that task. After the marriage, Valjean does confess his identity to Marius, but in so doing tells Marius only of the evil that he's done. It seems that Valjean still isn't convinced that he is truly capable of good. Valjean's confession repulses Marius, and Marius later acts in such a way as to discourage Valjean from seeing his adoptive daughter.

This breaks Valjean's heart, and his faith (and maybe his spirit) begins to slowly fade to the point of death.

Valjean feels that he has confessed everything to Marius, but this isn't the case. Is confession only the acknowledgment of faults? When we daily confess to God, are we only supposed to admit our shortfalls? Of course being honest about the ways in which we have not followed our calling, and the times we have not loved our neighbor in the way that Christ loves us, is certainly part of our daily prayer. Many would do well to acknowledge their imperfections, but we also have to be honest about the ways in which Christ has been working through us. Many would do well to recognize that they are capable of goodness. Sometimes the darkness is so great that we lose ourselves.

Valjean's confession isn't honest. Only confessing his sins is not the full picture of what God is doing in his life. While Valjean was in the sewers, he came across Thénardier, who yet again extorted Valjean. He thought Valjean was stealing trinkets from Marius, whom he presumed to be dead. To remember the encounter, Thénardier takes a piece from Marius's jacket in case he needs proof of Valjean's suspected thievery. This shred of proof meant for evil will eventually be used for good, or as we remember from Joseph's story in Genesis, "Even though you intended to do harm to me, God intended it for good" (Genesis 50:20a). Thénardier makes the mistake of trying to extort Marius by revealing the true identity of his father-in-law. He hopes to receive funds by keeping the secret that Valjean was stealing from the dead in the sewers, and when Thénardier shows Marius the cloth as proof, Marius finally discovers the truth that it was Valjean who saved his life.

Valjean's goodness is finally revealed. Marius and Cosette quickly rush to see Valjean, who by now is in a terrible state. There is a great reconciliation among the three, and Valjean experiences joy for the first time in his long life. Valjean tells Cosette about her mother, asks her to forgive the Thénardiers, and finally dies a happy man. Valjean finally experiences the peace that grace affords, and his conversion is complete. Although his story began with a grace offered, Valjean didn't quite understand the power of this grace until the end of the story. The same is often true for us. God's grace is profound. Grace is offered even before we are aware we are in need, it justifies us so that we can stop justifying ourselves, and it is the power of God to transform who we are. Sometimes this gift takes a lifetime to recognize.

2

WHEN GRACE AND JUSTICE COLLIDE: THE STORY OF JAVERT

"To feel emotion was terrible. To be carved in stone, the very figure of chastisement, and to discover suddenly under the granite of face something contradictory that is almost a heart."[1]

As Christians we are quite comfortable talking about God's love. According to First John, "God is love," and the way we experience this love is through grace. Scripture also talks about God's Law that was given to Moses, and God's justice rolling down like waters (Amos 5:24). What does it look like for grace and justice to occupy the same place at the same time? Psalm 30:5 gives us a glimpse at what this might mean: "[God's] anger is but for a moment; / his favor is for a lifetime." But is the expression of God's grace and justice more nuanced than this? If we assume that God's anger is expressed as justice and God's favor as God's love, we fall upon a slippery slope that dangerously suggests that God is rather fickle. Our understanding of grace and justice needs to be more nuanced than this.

The Gospels offer a more nuanced picture of what happens when grace and justice occupy the same space. In John chapter 8 we hear a story of a woman caught in the act of adultery. The crowd presents her before Jesus saying that the law of Moses demands that we stone her, and they aren't wrong, according to Leviticus 20:10 (although the law states that both the man and the woman shall be put to death and the man in this story is conspicuously absent). Jesus replies, "Let anyone among you who is without sin be the first to throw a stone at her." One by one they begin to walk away. Jesus approaches the woman and asks, "Where are they? Has no one condemned you?" . . . "Neither do I condemn you. Go your way, and from now on do not sin again" (John 8:7, 10, 11). In this story we see an amazing grace in Jesus withholding condemnation. We also see justice when Jesus reminds the crowd that it is unjust for the guilty to pass judgment on the guilty, or maybe more accurately, the powerful who have not been held accountable passing judgment upon the powerless is not how the law should be applied.

The Lenten season culminates in the ultimate expression of God's grace and justice in the same place. The cross is where grace and justice collide in the person of Jesus. God passes judgment on sin, revealing that sin leads to death, but there is grace because God in the flesh is the one who assumes this judgment. God reveals justice against our sin, and God offers grace by assuming the punishment in the divine self. For Police Inspector Javert, grace and justice can never occupy the same place because grace is a foolish human weakness that only destroys the justice humanity needs to survive.

BY THE LETTER, NOT THE SPIRIT

I have a love-hate relationship with computers. Computers are at their best with precision, repetition, and calculation. If you plug in the right numbers, the answer will be correct every time. I appreciate the red squiggles when a word is *Les Misspelled* and the notifications that pop up to remind me that I need to pick up snacks for my daughter's kindergarten class. Computers are supposed to do exactly what I'm asking them to do, but sometimes it seems that they're toying with me. Sometimes I click "print" and nothing happens. Occasionally my computer will connect with my Bluetooth speaker, and sometimes it won't. Every now and again my computer will just shut down, like a teenager when you've asked her to clean her room.

Victor Hugo presents Police Inspector Javert like a computer at its best. He is cold, calculating, and precise. He unwaveringly follows the letter of the law as if it is a programming code. If there is any variation to the code, the program doesn't work. For Javert, there is no room for improvisation, discernment, or compromise. There is only law or chaos, light or dark, and right or wrong. For example, Javert refers to Valjean as "Prisoner 24601." This offers us a quick glimpse into Javert's character. Names carry nuance, but numbers are absolute.

It's too simple to see Javert as the villain and Valjean as the hero. *Les Misérables* is much too complex to be boiled down to such a simple polarity. Javert is a beautiful foil to Valjean's seemingly murky morality. Javert is an antagonist for sure, but hardly a villain. Early in the story Javert is tasked with being the warden of a large prison camp, and a job such as this requires a type of order most of us cannot understand.

Order and rules are not bad things. Genesis 1 can be read as a story about bringing order to chaos. When the earth was a formless void, God created light to burn away the darkness, separated the chaotic waters, and formed the foundation upon which everything would be built. In order for life to be, there must be space for it to be. Think of it this way. We are embodied creations. Everything we know, experience, and share is incarnational—all in the context of our bodies. Our bodies are quite ordered, meaning that ideally our heart beats when it should, our lungs draw in air when they need to, and our white blood cells attack harmful pathogens and keep us healthy. When that order becomes chaotic, it's very difficult to think about anything other than our body. Try stubbing your toe and talking at the same time. Try brushing your teeth when your heart unexpectedly skips a beat. Try thinking about, well anything, when you are recovering in a hospital bed after surgery. There is a deep connection among our body, mind, and soul. When one is out of balance, the rest follow suit.

Order is helpful, and chaos can make life more difficult, but both in their extremes make the gospel difficult to live out and share. On the one hand, having too much order makes it extremely difficult to incorporate improvisation when met with the unexpected. Likewise, having not enough order makes even the simplest of tasks exhausting. As a pastor I certainly honor order, but I tend to lean into chaos, and according to some, too much chaos. For example, each Sunday when we share Holy Communion, my invitation is, "When the Holy Spirit invites you to the table, taste and see that the Lord is good." In other words, the ushers don't direct the worshipers when to come down to receive Communion, when to go back, and how to return to his or her pew. This wasn't the most popular decision I made early in my tenure in my congregation. The looks on their faces (and the emails that followed) were more than an indication that some were displeased.

But sometimes what seems to be chaos is quite a blessing. Once I had the time to explain why we made this change with the Holy Communion invitation (which I *should* have done before making the change itself), there was much less anxiety. Inviting people to move at the prompting of the Holy Spirit accomplishes two things. First, it adds a spiritual element to the act of coming forward that is hard to find when you're being told when to leave your pew. Sitting in prayer and coming to the table when you feel called by the Holy Spirit add beauty to the experience. Second, and much less theologically, it's a helpful practice for people who are new to your faith community. Even though we say that all are welcome to the table, it takes great courage to come down to the chancel rail the first time you enter into a sanctuary. This gives guests an opportunity to decline without the awkwardness of getting word to the usher at the end of the pew.

Javert would be very uncomfortable with the way we offer Communion. Justice, for Javert, is nearly the sole expression of "You reap what you sow," except the only way to make amends for wrongdoing is through penalty. Upon leaving M. Bienvenu's home where Valjean received grace for stealing his silver, Valjean steals a coin from Gervais, a young chimney sweep traveling the road. Interestingly, stealing this coin from the boy, as opposed to the silver from the priest, is what finally convinces Valjean to change his life. It was the realization that the temptation to steal was too deeply ingrained in his soul. The silver he had was more than he needed, yet he stole from the boy seemingly out of habit. It's like what St. Augustine said in his *Confessions*, written around AD 400: "I was in love with my own ruin, in love with decay: not with the thing for which I was falling into decay but with decay itself."[2]

The Pharisees have something in common with Javert. They hold an unapologetic love for order in the extreme. It's hard to blame them. They lived under the theological assumption that Israel's failure to keep the letter of the Law was why many of the Jewish people were sent into Babylonian exile. Upon their return to the land, there was a zealousness for keeping a strict adherence to the Law so that God would bless them to remain in the land. Like Javert, there is little room for compromise. If there were any acceptable exceptions to the lawful provisions, it would be included in the law itself. This is one of the reasons Jesus and the Pharisees were in such conflict. Jesus' ministry, on the whole, was a re-narration of the Law in order to bring about its completion. The problem was he didn't establish a new written law, and he based these new interpretations on his own authority. One person making seemingly situational decisions and judgments is a recipe for disaster, and so they plotted to destroy him.

Have you had experience with the tension between following the letter of the law versus the spirit of the law? We have a very sensible vacation policy for my staff. When we were amending our policy, we included a footnote that reads, "Additional PTO may be granted by the Lead Pastor." Even though our policy is quite specific in terms of amount of time one can be away and for what reasons, there should always be, written into the "law," an opportunity for improvisation. Sometimes people need a Sabbath day without the pressure of losing a day of vacation or sick leave. If they might have to change their family's vacation plans because work is stressful and they need some Sabbath time, they might not be honest about needing to step away.

Saying that Javert is a computer following a justice program isn't entirely true; at least this isn't where the story is headed. For now, this is where his character begins, but it doesn't take long for Javert's character to change, and initially, not for the better.

Searching

I remember when my wife and I were expecting our first child, and everything I would see around me pointed to this new life change. It seemed that every television commercial had something to do with diapers, I noticed sales in the local supermarket for baby formula, and I began to notice just how many people were driving around with car seats. This is actually an experience called the Baader-Meinhof Phenomenon. For example, let's say you've started reading this really cool book about the nature of grace in Victor Hugo's *Les Misérables*, and then you notice a radio commercial about the musical coming to town, and then you see an advertisement about the recent Masterpiece retelling of the story.

At first you think there is this great divine hand at work, or the cosmos is lining up together encouraging you to see the musical. But, sadly, this is just a coincidence—your brain is hard-wired to recognize patterns, even when patterns aren't really there. Our brains are so hungry to see patterns, we tend to hold a selective attention to things that seem unimportant. In other words, when we are primed to see something, we tend to ignore everything that isn't it.

For Inspector Javert, everything points to Jean Valjean. Every crime and every criminal seem to be linked to the escaped convict, which only leads Javert into a deeper obsession to find him. It almost seems that he is receiving a divine calling to bring him to justice. Javert hears about a kidnapping at the Thénardiers' inn and goes to investigate what he is sure has something to do with Valjean. Interestingly, he is correct in his assumption that Valjean is the one who had taken Cosette from the Thénardiers, but his obsession in seeing what he wants to see clouds his judgment about the facts of the case. On the one hand his penchant for noticing patterns makes him an excellent detective. Unfortunately, this also brings about a debilitating bias that propels him deeper into his obsession.

Our assumptions about the world make things simple. At best our assumptions help us quickly navigate the complex. For example, every time I get in the car to drive somewhere, I can assume that my car will accelerate and brake exactly as they have before. If I had to relearn how to drive every time I got in the car, being a parent of four kids would be even more exhausting than it already is. Being surprised every time you press the brake is certainly no way to spend an afternoon in the carpool.

Assumptions can be very helpful in navigating things, but assumptions are not always helpful when working with people. On the one hand, you probably have a pretty good idea how the people in your family around the dinner table are going to act on any given day. I know that smoked salmon will never be on the dinner menu because my kids will (almost) never eat fish. On the other hand, when we assume we know all there is to know about someone, we no longer value them as we should. Jesus plays with our assumptions time and time again in several of his parables. In the parable of the prodigal son, we assume that when the son returns he is going to become one of his father's hired hands. We assume that the Samaritan in the parable of the good Samaritan is anything but. When the publican and the sinner are praying (Luke 18:9-14), we assume that the publican will be the one who goes home justified. Jesus certainly surprises us. Of course, these parables aren't about us; rather they reveal the nature of God. These parables are surprising because far too often our assumptions about God are shortsighted and shallow and simply reveal a grander and seemingly more perfect picture of our self.

Lent is a time to set our assumptions aside, to lay down what we think we know about God, God's people, and God's world, so that we can be recalibrated, like setting the scale back to zero. This doesn't mean we forget what we have learned or throw away the formation into which we have lived. It's like when Jesus says, "You have heard that it was said, 'An eye for an eye and a tooth for a tooth.' But I say to you, Do not resist an evildoer" (Matthew 5:38-39). This particular teaching found in Exodus 21:24, Leviticus 24:20, and Deuteronomy 19:21 had an important function in the formation of the Jewish people. "An eye for an eye" is meant to reign in unjust retribution. If someone stole something from you, burning down all of his property was a punishment far greater than the crime committed. This kind of law would be fruitful in the context of *Les Misérables*. Jean Valjean initially served five years' hard labor for stealing bread. He eventually served nineteen years in prison because of his many attempted escapes.

Jesus was well aware of the Law. Saying "You have heard that it was said, . . . but I say to you" is not a means of throwing away the Law or treating it as unimportant. In a way, Jesus is recalibrating us to God's will by setting the Law on the scales of his own divine authority and setting the counter to God's intention as a zero point. Of course this is risky. Jesus continues saying, "But if anyone strikes you on the right cheek, turn the other also; and if anyone wants to sue you and take your coat, give your cloak as well" (Matthew 5:39-40). Jesus' re-narration of the Law is completely foreign to Javert. Turning the other cheek is at best a sign of weakness, and at worst a slippery slope toward chaos.

Recalibration is not what Javert has in mind. He cannot see the potential good of what Valjean has done in taking Cosette away from Thénardier; rather Valjean has again escaped paying for his crimes. There is no good that can atone for lawlessness in Javert's view. So, he begins to search for Valjean like a bloodhound. He becomes obsessed with bringing Valjean to justice, and this obsession has made him blind to the grace that should be offered. For Javert, a good end can never justify breaking the rules along the way. Of course, living out the gospel can sometimes appear to be breaking the rules for all of the right reasons.

In Disguise

In eighth grade I wrote a very dark poem for an end-of-the-semester poetry project. I had quickly learned that if a poem were happy or if it rhymed the letter grade would be low. So I wrote a dark, brooding, "emo" poem titled, "Matt's Mask." In it I talked about how every day I put on a mask to hide my true self. The world was dark, and the only joy to be had was rooted in deception, which was very different from the comical limericks I was used to composing. After reading the poem my teacher alerted the school counselor. She called me into her dimly lit beige office, sat me down on the couch, held my hand, and asked me if I was OK. I said, "Yeah." She replied, "I heard about your poem. Do you want to talk about it?" I asked, "Sure. Did I get an A?" Confused, she answered, "I don't know." I said, "I wrote a limerick about Hillary Clinton and got a C. Then I wrote a poem about darkness swallowing the earth and I got an A. So did I get an A?" The counselor quickly figured out what was going on and sent me back to class. The poem wasn't about who I was; rather it was a means of giving the teacher what she wanted. Ironically, I *was* wearing a mask. It wasn't a happy face disguising my deep sadness, but a faux sadness masking my desire for a good grade.

It seems that Javert would honor integrity above all else, but this isn't entirely true. You might think that a character so dedicated to the rule of law could never justify bending the rules in order to bring about justice, but when Javert runs into difficulty finding Valjean, he begins a slow descent into deception. Hugo artfully represents this change in Javert's character by literally having him wear a disguise. Javert receives word that there is a new man in Paris who often gives beggars alms during his evening walks. Because of Javert's obsession, he assumes that this new stranger is Valjean. One evening Javert disguises himself as a beggar, and his suspicions are confirmed when Valjean unknowingly offers Javert some coins. A few days later, Valjean notices Javert's menacing silhouette approaching his humble residence, so he and Cosette quickly leave again, escaping Javert's pursuit.

This deception might seem small to the rest of us, but this is only the beginning of Javert's descent. This is not unlike King Saul's descent from ruler to charlatan in First Samuel. This story begins when the people of Israel demand a king, not so that they might have a representative before God, but so that they might be like the other nations. God grants their wish, but warns them that having a Lord other than the Lord will be a decision fraught with misery. Nevertheless, Samuel, God's prophet, anoints Saul as king, and he rules God's people. It wasn't long before Saul began to turn away from God's commands and becomes a selfish, wicked ruler, falling deeper and deeper into darkness.

First Samuel 28 is a story in four acts. In the first act, Saul is nervous, fearful, and desperate on the eve of meeting the Philistines for battle. Early in the chapter the narrator sets the stage. Samuel is dead, Saul has expelled the mediums and wizards, Saul is afraid, and God is silent. In the next three scenes, all of these proclamations will be turned upside down.

God's silence sets the action in motion. When Saul saw the army of the Philistines, he was afraid, and his heart trembled greatly, so he prayed to God, but received no answer, neither by dreams nor Urim nor prophet. So, he gathered his stewards together and asked them to seek out a medium so that he might have an answer. The story is already beginning to turn on itself. First, Saul pronounced the expulsion of the witches and mediums so, supposedly, there are no mediums with whom to consult. Second, Saul is dissatisfied with God's silence. Ironically, Saul hadn't been listening to God when God was speaking. God's words weren't good enough, and now God's silence is unnerving.

As the curtain rises on scene two, Saul's men find a medium in the woods of Endor. Saul takes off his kingly garment and puts on "other clothes." The Hebrew term for "other clothes" essentially means "treachery." Saul's kingship is unraveling before the audience's eyes. He pronounces a rule that neither he nor anyone else follows, God becomes silent, and he takes off his kingly effects and puts on treachery. Saul has lost all authority and power, and the clothes he has put on are the identity he has now assumed.

Javert disguising himself as a beggar in order to bring Valjean to justice is like King Saul taking off his kingly garments and hiding himself in order to find solace on the eve of battle. Have you ever "disguised" yourself? Have you ever hidden something about yourself in order to reach a desired conclusion? It could have been a small thing like feigning interest in a meeting with your boss so that the meeting will conclude more quickly, or pretending to be interested in a friend's conversation so that there won't be awkward silence. Have you ever hidden some pretty big things? Maybe you've been spending more money than you know your spouse would like, or maybe those innocent text messages aren't so innocent anymore. Sometimes our self-deception seems well intentioned, but it doesn't take long for us to lose ourselves and become someone we never thought we would be.

I remember in divinity school several of my friends and I tried to fast on Wednesdays and Fridays during the Lenten season. With the help of a community, it was easy to accomplish at first, but soon the newness wore off and it became difficult to keep the practice going. The hunger pangs, headaches, and obsession over the next meal became distracting enough for me to stop. One of our professors had emphasized the importance of fasting as a spiritual discipline during weekly worship. He mentioned that we too often mask who we are with food. Never truly being hungry was a satiation that can sometimes hide our true identity. It's difficult to know what the soul needs when the soul is hidden. In other words, were we grumpy because we hadn't eaten, or were we grumpy by default and our comfort masked it?

Javert begins to backslide, as it were, slipping into disguises to hide himself in order to bring Valjean to justice. Could it be that his reliance on justice through the status his office affords has been his mask hiding his true depravity, or is the story more conventional in the sense that this disguise is a metaphor for losing his identity? Ultimately our interpretation may not matter, other than to recognize that Javert is changing, and not for the better.

DECEPTION

My oldest daughter has always had a flair for the dramatic. It is both a blessing and a curse to know that she is exactly like me when I was her age. One afternoon when picking Isabelle up from first-grade carpool we noticed that she was wearing a new pair of glasses. We were surprised because neither did she need glasses, nor had we given them to her. She told us that she had trouble reading her schoolwork, so her teacher sent her to the office where the school nurse fitted her for reading glasses. The story sounded suspicious, namely due to the fact that the glasses had no lenses. My wife and I chuckled and thought little about it until two weeks later when she was still wearing them. She put on her glasses first thing in the morning and only took them off when going to bed. She would take them off, pretending to clean the nonexistent lenses, and while they were off she would squint and walk into walls. To say that she was fully committed to this vision-impaired character she was portraying would be a laughable understatement. After three weeks of her unbroken character, my wife and I became mildly anxious. We appreciated her magnificent imagination, but it was time for our daughter to join the real world again.

Unexpectedly, one day we noticed she wasn't wearing her glasses. We asked her why she wasn't wearing them, and she replied that today was church picture day, and the glasses were hiding her face. I suppose when all else fails, lean in to vanity to get the job done. But then she started to cry. She admitted that she had told us a "whopper." She didn't have trouble reading her classwork. Her teacher didn't send her to the office. She's never met the school nurse. She got the glasses out of the treasure box in class and simply wanted to wear them. I certainly hope that my daughter uses her imaginative superpower for good one day.

There can be a fine line between pretending and deception. It's fun to be an actor in a play, but you have to know when the show is over. If the stage proscenium extends into the real world, you can lose yourself. When Javert consistently fails in apprehending Valjean through disguise and midnight meanderings, he chooses to take things one step further. When the students in Paris gather arms and build barricades to militantly resist the government during the uprising of 1832, Javert becomes a spy and joins their ranks. He no longer is wearing a disguise; rather he is living under a created persona. Javert, who honors the rule of law above all else, is now throwing away the very integrity he has offered his life to serve.

Valjean has been living under a pseudonym for most of the story in order to escape a punitive justice, and now Javert is following suit. With great irony, Javert is becoming what he has fought against, but is there a moral equivalence between what Valjean and Javert are doing? Is deception, whatever the reason, a sin? *Les Misérables* actually begins with deception for the good.

M. Bienvenu chooses to tell the local police that he gave Valjean the silver he had stolen as a gift. This misdirection for the good sets the tone for the rest of Valjean's life. He never shies away from hiding the truth, if hiding the truth leads to the good, or as Bonhoeffer wrote—"Treating truthfulness as a principle leads . . . to the grotesque conclusion that if asked by a murderer whether my friend, whom he was pursuing, had sought refuge in my house, I would have to answer honestly in the affirmative. Here the self-righteousness of conscience has escalated into blasphemous recklessness and become an impediment to responsible action."[3]

Jesus' parable of the dishonest steward is a troubling passage (read Luke 16:1-15). It says there was a rich man who had a manager, and charges were brought to him that this man was squandering his property. So the rich man summoned his manager and said to him, "What is this that I hear about you? Give me an accounting of your management, because you cannot be my manager any longer." Then the manager said to himself, "What will I do?" He goes to the first of his master's debtors and says, "How much do you owe my master?" One hundred jugs of oil? Quickly change that to fifty, he says. The steward goes to the second and says, "And how much do you owe?" One hundred containers of wheat? Quickly change that to eighty, he says. He brings this back to his master and he is commended.

This parable is troubling, at least, if we're thinking about worldly economy. This story is about economics, but as a means of putting your house in order with God at the center. Look closely at what the manager says to himself in verse 4: "I have decided what to do so that, when I am dismissed as manager, people may welcome me into their homes." Being welcomed into a home is an important phrase found twice in the parable. In essence, this parable is not about numbers or commerce; rather it is about changing economies, or "households."

What is happening in this story is a transformation of economies. Worldly economics, or *mammon*, survives off of scarcity—the assumption that there isn't enough to go around. The other economy at work in this story is *manna*—the abundance that God provides. This story is about two economies coming to blows, and the shrewd manager is caught in the middle. When mammon has him dismissed, he trades it for manna. As Sam Wells, former dean of Duke Chapel (Durham, North Carolina) and now vicar of St. Martin-in-the-Fields (London), put it, "He realizes the friends are more important than the money—or even the job. He moves from mammon to manna, from an economy of scarcity and perpetual anxiety to an economy of abundance and limitless grace."[4] He no longer needs to live off the debt of other. He has found friendship. Listen to the words of the parable—"And I tell you, make friends for yourselves by means of [mammon] so that when it is gone [not if, *when* it fails you], they may welcome you into the eternal homes" (verse 9).

Although both Valjean and Javert use deception, they are working within two different economies. Telling the truth is less about conveying fact than it is about creating an economy in which abundant life can flourish. Valjean is constantly on the move, hiding his identity in order to protect others. Javert, on the other hand, has become a spy across enemy lines under a misguided sense of justice. Javert will soon discover that what he has known as justice is unveiled as scarcity. There is no room for criminals and the righteous to be at the same table. There can only be a few at the top to bring order to the many. Ultimately, Javert's assumption of scarcity will buckle under the abundance of grace Valjean offers. He assumes that the world is not big enough for both him and Valjean, and this will lead to his self-inflicted demise.

56

The Rejection of Grace

Javert was born in prison to criminal parents. The stark, cold reality of prison being the only narrative he knew propelled him into a world of absolutes. One will either prey on the world or be charged with ordering it. Interestingly Valjean struggles with the same view. Both characters struggle with redemption's possibility. Valjean believes redemption is possible, though he constantly questions his own merit. Javert never questions his merit while assuming that real change is never possible. In this way, Valjean and Javert are foils to one another. Both have experienced a form of Hell, and both have ordered their lives never to return. They diverge in only one way—Valjean has received redemption, and Javert is trying to earn it.

Javert's obsession with the law is his way of crucifying his past. He is ashamed of who he was and therefore zealously fights against it. Have you ever been with someone who was just like you? Often someone with your own quirks, successes, and failures is someone you don't readily get along with. It is difficult to have patience with someone who has made your same mistakes. Loving your neighbor isn't easy when your neighbor holds your same sins. Javert hates his former life and therefore hates criminals. He lives under the assumption that redemption is impossible, which means deep down he hates himself. It's a hate that he believes will never go away. In his mind, his adherence to the law is like hanging off the edge of a cliff. If you lose your grip for even a moment, you will plummet. The problem is, he doesn't see that there is a walking path just under his feet. In other words, Valjean and Javert see each other eye to eye, but one is hanging by his fingertips and the other is standing on the solid ground of grace.

When the uprising of 1832 begins, Valjean and Javert find each other behind the barricades with the student revolutionaries, albeit for different reasons. Javert has entered the ranks as a spy to bring the revolutionaries to justice. Valjean's appearance is much more ambiguous. Hugo never quite explains why Valjean decides to don a National Guard uniform to find his way into the skirmish. It could be that he wants to save Marius, his daughter Cosette's love interest. It also could be that he wants to see Marius die with his own eyes, ensuring that he won't take away the only thing that Valjean has grown to love. Regardless, both men meet once again, and this meeting will lead to Javert's demise.

Javert is quickly discovered as a spy and is held hostage by the students. When it becomes obvious that their revolution will end in a disheartening and overwhelming defeat, Enjorlas, the leader of the rebels, orders Javert to be executed. Valjean volunteers and takes Javert away to end his life. While out of sight of the barricades, Valjean cuts Javert's restraints, announces that he is free, and then gives Javert his pseudonym and address so that he may take him away to prison. Javert is in disbelief. He begs Valjean to exact his revenge, but Valjean refuses. As Javert walks away free, Valjean fires his pistol in the air and tells Enjolras that the deed has been done.

This is a grace Javert cannot stomach. Letting Valjean go free is something that cannot exist in Javert's worldview. Valjean has proven that Javert's understanding of absolutes is wrong. Redemption is possible, criminals are capable of good, and Javert simply cannot live with himself. Has your worldview ever radically changed? Have you been living your life under one set of rules to discover later that you weren't as enlightened as you thought? Growing pains hurt. Sometimes we understand Scripture as more or less a rulebook full of guidelines that, if followed appropriately, would lead to heaven as a reward. After studying, meditating, and diving into God's Word, we discover that God's revelation to us is much more nuanced, layered, complex, and beautiful than a list of "shalls" and "shall nots." It is more living water than instruction manual.

Of course, Scripture is useful for teaching (2 Timothy 3:16), and we should know and understand God's word well, but I had it backwards. I was searching for Christ through the Scriptures instead of allowing Christ to bring the Scriptures alive. It's like an oft-quoted story I recently read: "There's an old story about a man who approached his pastor and said, 'I do not mean to boast, but I consider myself quite a learned man. I have read through the entire Bible three times.' The pastor smiled, nodded, and said, 'That is admirable, my friend. But tell me, how much of the Bible has been through you?'"

Has your worldview radically changed? If it hasn't, then maybe there's some work to be done. A few years ago I met with a man in my office who was working through new questions. He was a great supporter of a strict immigration policy that enforced a zero-tolerance policy toward deporting undocumented workers. But then it was discovered that one of his colleagues with whom he had been working for decades was undocumented. He told me that this was a man who was a hard worker who was putting food on the table for his family, paying his taxes, and never strayed from company policy. He then told me he wasn't so sure about his understanding of immigration. He then asked me the best question I've been asked in quite some time: "Is my view changing because of the Holy Spirit, or am I acquiescing simply because I know this man and see what a hard worker he is?" It is a beautiful question, and I would argue that the answer is yes. This is why loving God and loving our neighbor is so important. Our love of God informs our love of neighbor, and our love of neighbor offers a holy context to our love of God. This love is who Jesus was—fully human and fully divine—God with a face. It is fascinating to see how our relationships inform how we understand the world. Of course, the next step is to hold compassion for a neighbor even if he isn't a hard worker or a family man or hasn't paid his taxes.

This is the kind of grace that Javert simply cannot understand, though interestingly he reciprocates. After Valjean drags Marius through the sewers in order to save his life, Javert meets him at the sewer's exit. Valjean assumes that Javert is there to apprehend him. He asks Javert to afford him to opportunity to save Marius's life, and surprisingly, Javert lets him and even calls his carriage to take them to Marius's grandfather's house. Valjean makes another request to see Cosette before he goes to prison, and again Javert agrees. Slowly Javert walks to a bridge overlooking the Seine. While watching the waters swirl, he wrestles with what to do. To apprehend Valjean would show a great dishonor to the man who saved his life. To let Valjean go free would be an incomprehensible breach of duty. There is only one way he can find peace in the midst of this perceived impasse. He climbs a bridge parapet and leaps into the river, ending his life. Javert is his own Judas. He feels that he has betrayed himself, and like Judas, in a way, he throws himself into the field of blood never to return (Acts 1:18-19).

3

THE POOR ARE ALWAYS WITH YOU: THE STORY OF FANTINE

"It is a terrible place, the pit of darkness, the stronghold of the blind. It is the threshold of the abyss."[1]

One of the main characters that affects everything in the story doesn't have a name. This character ties all of the other characters together. To some this character is avoided at all costs, for others it is the catalyst for revolution. This character is poverty itself. Both Valjean and Javert have known the grip of poverty, but for most of the story they are men of great means. Valjean uses his wealth with great generosity, while Javert constantly distances himself from the poor—whom he sees as less than human and deserving of their miserable state. Poverty directly drives the story of four characters in *Les Misérables*, though each has a very particular relationship with what Jesus says "will always be with us."

What does Jesus mean when he says that the poor will always be with us? Each Gospel presents this peculiar teaching with a particular flavor. Matthew and Mark suggest that the point is remembering the generosity of an unnamed woman who offered Jesus more than the disciples could imagine (Matthew 26:13; Mark 14:7). This story is about the nature of forgiveness from Luke's point of view (Luke 7:36-50). John offers identity to the unnamed characters in the other Gospels, suggesting that Jesus' teaching was a reprimand against Judas because he held scorn for Mary's close relationship with Jesus.

Maybe the point of it all is to remember Deuteronomy 15:10-11: "Give liberally and be ungrudging when you do so. . . . Since there will never cease to be some in need on the earth, I therefore command you, 'Open your hand to the poor and needy neighbor in your land.'" In other words, the disciples seem quite concerned with how the woman is using her gifts with no consideration as to how they are using their own. However we are called to best understand this teaching, the truth is we all have a brother or sister in need, and at some point we, ourselves, will be in need. Just as the Gospels offer this story in slightly different flavors, the characters in *Les Misérables* each respond to the human invention of poverty in slightly different ways.

WHEN DREAMS BECOME NIGHTMARES

Almost every summer I have the blessing to accompany our youth on their annual mission to the Navajo Nation in Kaibeto, Arizona. Living in Louisiana and being mostly surrounded by water, the mountains and arid landscape pull me to notice even the smallest details of my surroundings. One year I had to cut my time short with the youth group. I flew in late to meet them several days into the trip, and I had to fly out early to prepare for an upcoming conference. My soul felt hurried and scattered, and the landscape was less awe-inspiring as it was a representation of the wilderness into which the Spirit drove Jesus. I felt as dry as the rusty soil.

We always end our time in Arizona at a beautiful natural landmark called Horseshoe Bend. This rock formation carved from the frigid river below is magnificent to see. That year, seeing the splendor of the U-shaped monolith offered me a hope that I desperately needed. Around the work sites, amidst the dust and the sparse vegetation, it is easy for you to lose sight of beauty. Seeing the sun set behind the bend felt like a chilly rain upon parched land.

When Fantine, a young, attractive, and naïve young woman, enters Hugo's story, it seems as if she will become a symbol of hope—much like the priest who offers Valjean a new life-giving path. It is easy to assume that she will perhaps cross paths with Valjean and offer him hopeful respite in his struggle to find redemption. Their paths do indeed cross, and there is hope to be found, but this hope will be foreign to Fantine. It isn't long before this narrative spark of life is completely destroyed by the human depravity she does not deserve. For Fantine, there is no Horseshoe Bend. There is no beauty offering life-giving water. This miserable soul will come only to know pain, despair, and a tragic death.

The *Les Misérables* musical introduces Fantine as a factory worker desperate to make ends meet in order to send much needed funds for her child, who is under an innkeeper's care. But this is not where her story begins. In Hugo's novel, Fantine is a picture of nineteenth-century French romanticism. She comes from modest beginnings but also enjoys the freedom and leisure of the upper class. In 1817, Fantine and several other ingénues enjoy a summer of frivolity, and she falls in love with Felix, a young aristocrat who sweeps her off her feet. Fantine and Felix become lovers, and they have a child, Cosette, together. It isn't long before Felix, wanting not to be burdened with the responsibility of fatherhood, leaves Fantine with nothing and returns to his parents' estate.

Fantine's heart is broken, but she is strong. She decides to leave and find work in Montreuil. On the way to start a new life, she seeks lodging in the Thénardiers' inn. Knowing that it will be difficult to find work as a single mother, she asks Thénardier and his wife to keep Cosette until she has secured employment and housing for the two of them. To say that this is a difficult decision isn't adequate, but the economic reality of nineteenth-century France gives her little choice. Some may even treat Fantine with disdain for making such a decision, but we would also need to share our scorn with Moses' mother, Jochebed (Exodus 6:20).

When the ancient Israelites became enslaved in Egypt, Pharaoh proclaimed that any male children born should be put to death. Moses' mother hid Moses for three months, but when she could no longer hide him, she put him in a basket and placed him in the Nile river. The biblical story doesn't offer any kind of inner monologue or rationale as to why Jochebed made such a risky decision. We can assume that because she lined the basket with pitch to keep it afloat, she was hoping that Moses would quickly be found. But there were no guarantees that Moses would be safe.

Do you know anyone who has had to make the difficult decision to place her child in the care of someone else? Do you know a family eager to open their home in hospitality? How does your faith community respond? I am thankful that our faith community has the Louisiana Methodist Children's Home less than an hour away. They provide an incredible ministry that offers housing to over one hundred children, life skills training, family counseling, and so much more. I have church members and clergy colleagues who have opened their life to welcome a child. One of my church members described being a foster and adoptive parent saying, "You realize love isn't based on DNA, but on quality time spent together." How does your faith community recognize that love isn't based on DNA? Is your community a champion of adoption? Maybe your church understands that, regardless of our ideas about immigration, families need to stay together? When Jesus tells the crowd that his family is those who do the Father's will, how do we put into practice the reality that family means more than those to whom we are related?

Regretfully, Fantine leaves Cosette behind and finds work in M. Madeleine's (Jean Valjean's) factory. It isn't long before Thénardier begins to extort Fantine for greater and greater funds, pretending that Cosette is ill. Fantine loses her position in the factory when it is discovered that she has a child, and she slips deeper and deeper into debt. In order to pay Thénardier's exorbitant requests, Fantine first sells her hair, then she sells her teeth, and finally she sells her body as a prostitute. Her spirit is crushed. It is difficult to recognize the free-spirited young woman who first entered our story.

Some say that God doesn't give you more than you can handle, but this is a lie. First, this terrible saying suggests that it is God doling out the difficulty, and it excuses Thénardier from being the monster that he is. Second, thinking that God doesn't give us more than we can handle doesn't lead us into asking the difficult questions as to why a single mother would have to lie about having a child in order to find a suitable job, why she has to offer everything she has to fulfill false debts, and why the city as a whole doesn't seem to care. For the citizens of Montreuil (and many who live in our own neighborhoods), poverty is punishment for poor choices, and the depravity is deserved. This is not the gospel. In Matthew 25, Jesus offers the parable of the sheep and goats, saying:

> *"Then he will say to those at his left hand, 'You that are accursed, depart from me into the eternal fire prepared for the devil and his angels; for I was hungry and you gave me no food, I was thirsty and you gave me nothing to drink, I was a stranger and you did not welcome me, naked and you did not give me clothing, sick and in prison and you did not visit me.' Then they . . . will answer, 'Lord, when was it that we saw you hungry or thirsty or a stranger or naked or sick or in prison, and did not take care of you?' Then he will answer them, 'Truly I tell you, just as you did not do it to one of the least of these, you did not do it to me.' And these will go away into eternal punishment, but the righteous into eternal life." (Matthew 25:41-46)*

There certainly are consequences for our actions. According to this parable, the consequences are great in turning a blind eye to the poor.

Fantine becomes the first of "the miserables" in our story. This young ingénue with such a hopeful future eventually dies under the weight of despair and poverty. She is abused, oppressed, and destroyed. But even in the depth of despair, there is still hope. Valjean finds Cosette and raises her as his own, and her story is one that ends well.

SURVIVAL OF THE FITTEST

"Why do bad things happen to good people?" might be a question we would ask about Fantine's story. "Why do good things happen to bad people?" we might initially ask about Thénardier. Thénardier is a cheat, swindler, and crook who will stop at nothing to survive. When Fantine finds herself in the grip of poverty, she offers herself for little in return. Thénardier, it seems, offers nothing and gets everything. Early in the story he seems to be a successful innkeeper and compassionate man who offers lodging and safety to any passersby, which is why Fantine feels confident she can leave Cosette in his care. Quickly we discover that Thénardier is nothing more than a con artist.

Looks can be deceiving. When Jesus spoke out against the Pharisees, he said, "Woe to you, scribes and Pharisees, hypocrites! For you are like whitewashed tombs, which on the outside look beautiful, but inside they are full of the bones of the dead and of all kinds of filth. So you also on the outside look righteous to others, but inside you are full of hypocrisy and lawlessness" (Matthew 23:27-28). Thénardier is not who he appears to be, but hiding behind a persona is a theme for many of the characters in this story. Valjean hides behind a pseudonym for most of the story; but regardless of his name, his actions reveal the goodness of his true nature. Javert puts on a disguise to become a spy, which symbolically reveals that he is losing his identity. In the case of Thénardier, he attempts to present himself as better than he is, though his depraved motivation never changes. He may appear to be always willing to help those in need, but inside he is full of hypocrisy and lawlessness.

I love how the musical introduces M. and Mme. Thénardier. On the surface he seems to be a man of charm and hospitality, but the music tells a different story. The music is in 2/4 time, which can symbolize a military march or great formal fanfare, but an oboe "slinks" about suggesting a false and bombastic buffoonery. The march reminds us that in the Hugo story, Thénardier presents himself as a war hero, but the "lazy" pomp of the orchestra pokes fun at this outrageous persona. It's like the hymn "Go to Dark Gethsemane." The lyrics and the music tell different stories. The lyrics, written by James Montgomery in the seventeenth century, detail Jesus' arrest, crucifixion, and resurrection, but the music is a sober and pleasing tune. The third stanza makes for a perfect Good Friday hymn:

Calvary's mournful mountain climb;
there, adoring at his feet,
mark the miracle of time,
God's own sacrifice complete.
"It is finished!" hear him cry;
learn of Jesus Christ to die.[2]

You are singing about Jesus' death on the cross in a major key, with an almost defiantly triumphant melody. By the time you arrive at the last stanza proclaiming Jesus' resurrection, the melody makes sense, but it takes time for the story to unfold. Much like the song that introduces Thénardier, the music foreshadows what the audience will realize before the characters on the stage understand. Thénardier is the "master" of the inn, but he also waters down drinks, uses fillers in the meat, steals money when patrons are drunk, and even calculates obscene charges for looking in the mirror more than once.

Several children live under the Thénardiers' care. Their own daughter, Eponine, enjoys the fruit of any luxury they have to offer. She is dressed in the finest clothing, is excused from daily chores, and is unmistakably their favorite. Cosette, on the other hand, is abused and treated with scorn. On Christmas Eve the inn is busier than normal, and Mme. Thénardier sends Cosette out into the dark and cold evening to fetch more water for the passersby. As you might imagine, Cosette is filled with a desperate fear of the dark. During the day she can see the abuse coming. At night, her fear becomes paralyzing.

Are you afraid of the dark? It's OK to admit it. I think we all are to some degree. At least, we seem to want to illuminate the darkness to such a degree that we've washed out the stars in the sky. I've never been a great fan of the dark. My imagination gets the better of me. Not being able to see what's in front of me causes me to assume the worst. When I was in youth group, we used to play a game where we would close our eyes and try to walk through a maze with only the voice of a friend to guide us. At best, this game teaches us to listen well and to trust the voice we hear, usually in conjunction with the "Good Shepherd" passages in John's Gospel. Little did I know for what this game was really preparing me.

During the summer going into the eighth grade, our youth group took a trip to the Cumberland Caverns. We decided to take the "Wild Tour," which was a four-hour spelunking tour through the caverns. They warned us that several spots on the tour were difficult and would require using our ears in addition to our eyes to find our way through. I was nervous about going, namely because I was always overweight as a kid, and the nooks and crannies seemed to be a tight fit. Never mind the fact that our tour guide said that if we got stuck, the best solution was to turn around and go back, rather than to force our way through somewhere we didn't fit. Nevertheless, peer pressure is a great motivator, so I grabbed my flashlight, put on my mildew-smelling helmet, and joined the group.

The first three and a half hours of the tour were actually a lot of fun. I marveled at the large caverns we were able to see, and I felt a sense of curiosity about exactly how the meandering twists and turns could have been formed. Then we reached the last part of the expedition—Hourglass Pass, appropriately named for the shape of the narrow passage through which we would need to pass in order to exit the tour. Our guide told us that we would either have to climb above or below the passage because the middle quickly became too narrow to pass through. We started down this final passageway, and I could literally see the light at the end of the tunnel. I was so thankful that the tour was almost over that I forgot to hoist myself above the increasingly narrow middle portion of the tunnel. I got to a point that I no longer could fold my body to army crawl under the encroaching walls. Finally, I twisted my body to the point where my arms had become pinned to my side with my flashlight pointing toward the cavern floor. I couldn't move in any direction. I was stuck.

My heart started pounding. I started to sweat. I had visions of being trapped forever, or at least until the next tour group arrived, which certainly would be after I had starved to death. I yelled "I'm stuck" as loud as I could, with no answer in return. Thankfully David, one of my friends in the group, was behind me on the tour. I told him that I was stuck and couldn't move, so he put his feet in the small of my back and kicked me through Hourglass Pass until I could free myself. I exited the tour with tears streaming down my face and a newly discovered fear of dark and enclosed spaces.

I can hardly write about this experience without having flashbacks. I can't imagine what it must be like for those who know a real evil that darkness can bring. Thénardier spends most of his time throughout the story under the cover of darkness. The dark is a means of hiding the abuse and violence he inflicts on everyone around him, and so Cosette finds herself in constant fear when there is no light to show the way. Thankfully, a mysterious traveler meets her while she is retrieving water from a nearby spring. He walks with her back to the inn, which staves off her fear. Of course, this mysterious figure is Jean Valjean, and it seems that either fate or providence has brought them together.

Maybe our collective fear of the dark is rooted in our fear of being alone? The game I played in youth group does teach an important lesson. God is always calling our name. God is always reminding us of God's divine presence. No matter how dark things may seem, or how alone we may feel, the Good Shepherd and Gatekeeper is relentlessly seeking for us—

"Very truly, I tell you, anyone who does not enter the sheep-fold by the gate but climbs in by another way is a thief and a bandit. The one who enters by the gate is the shepherd of the sheep. The gatekeeper opens the gate for him, and the sheep hear his voice. He calls his own sheep by name and leads them out. When he has brought out all his own, he goes ahead of them, and the sheep follow him because they know his voice." (John 10:1-4)

Thénardier is always trying to climb into the sheepfold by "another way." Unlike Valjean, who struggles daily to offer grace, Thénardier is constantly looking for the path of least resistance. His constant attempt to sneak into the sheepfold perpetuates a necessity to pretend being something that he isn't, and eventually his deception will cause him to lose even the little that he has.

YOU REAP WHAT YOU SOW?

One of my favorite songs to listen to when I'm having a bad day is "You Get What You Give" by the New Radicals. It's just a little reminder that no matter how difficult the day has been, serving and giving ourselves to the work of the church offers a great reward. It's like the musical version of "Do not be deceived; God is not mocked, for you reap whatever you sow" (Galatians 6:7). This is a fine verse to hold on to, but sometimes Scripture can offer a confusing picture about the relationship between good works and the reward we receive. Psalm 73:3 says, "For I was envious of the arrogant; / I saw the prosperity of the wicked." Jesus says, "For [God] makes his sun rise on the evil and on the good, and sends rain on the righteous and on the unrighteous" (Matthew 5:45).

Do we get what we deserve? Have you ever been jealous of those who have made poor decisions, and yet everything seems to work out? Have you felt that no good deed goes unpunished?

Les Misérables, the musical, aggravates our notion of "you reap what you sow." By the end of the show, the Thénardiers seem to have prospered. We find them at Marius and Cosette's wedding rubbing elbows with the French elite. Their lying, cheating, and thievery results in wealth and the reward of the "good life."

But then they fade from the story, and we return to seeing Jean Valjean near death singing a most beautiful line, and the most important lesson in the musical: "To love another person is to see the face of God."[3] Although on the surface it may seem that the Thénardiers reaped what they did not sow, if we dig a bit deeper we will recognize that their temporal wealth and easy living pale in comparison to the love that Valjean has discovered as he breathes his last. The same holds true with Psalm 73. Though it begins with the poet grieving over how the wicked prosper, by the end we read, "Indeed, those who are far from you will perish; / you put an end to those who are false to you. / But for me it is good to be near God; / I have made the Lord GOD my refuge, / to tell of all your works" (Psalm 73:27-28).

Hugo's story offers a more conventional approach to getting what one deserves. Not long after Valjean pays the Thénardiers 1,500 francs to take Cosette under his care, they fall into bankruptcy and lose the inn. They travel to Paris, where they attempt to make ends meet by leading a band of thieves to rob and extort anyone foolish enough to cross their path. They are constantly in need because their ill-gotten gains are spent as quickly as they are received. It is not their poverty that places them among the wicked in Hugo's story, as we will later discover with the redeemed tragedy of the Thénardiers' children Gavroche and Eponine; rather it is their spiritual shallowness, greed, and moral depravity Hugo reveals to be their failing.

The Thénardiers are "hungry ghosts." Imagine a ghost of a person, someone you can clearly see through, whose motives are rarely virtuous. He has a voracious appetite, and he is never satisfied. He has a neck the width of a pencil and a mouth the size of a pin's head. Even if you tried to feed him with good things, he would not be able to swallow them. "Hungry ghosts" are exhausting because they never offer anything and always ask for everything. Do you have someone in your story who is a "hungry ghost"? The only time they call is when they are in need. There is a great episode of *The Fresh Prince of Bel-Air* that explains just what a hungry ghost is. Will, played by Will Smith, reunites with his father, Lou, who had left Will and his mother when Will was a child. At first it seems that the relationship is heading toward reconciliation, but it isn't long before Lou begins asking for help. Lou makes shallow promises that Will wants to believe, but in the end his father makes excuses and leaves Will's life for good. Will's monologue at the end of the episode is arguably one of the most moving soliloquies in television and reveals the pain of what happens when a hungry ghost hovers too long around the people the ghost seemingly loves. When I counsel people, I rarely advocate for severing a relationship, but a hungry ghost only knows how to take. If a hungry ghost goes unchecked, he will consume everything, even the people he loves.

Hugo's presentation of the Thénardiers is a cautionary tale for those who only know how to take. Thénardier slips deeper and deeper into debt and squalor until we finally see him in the sewers sifting for trinkets among human waste. I'm not sure how best to explain what hitting rock bottom feels like, but being up to your knees in excrement hoping to find gold in a pitch-black sewer might be the best explanation I've read. And yet there is still goodness to be found, although this was not Thénardier's intent. Thénardier happens across Valjean carrying Marius through the sewers to bring him to safety. He thinks he has found a fellow thief stealing money off a dead man and tries to use this encounter to his advantage. He tries to extort Valjean for money, saying that for a price he will show Valjean the way out of the sewers. Valjean has very little to give, so Thénardier takes a portion of Marius's coat for collateral in case he might later be able to use this meeting to his advantage. Later in the story, Thénardier tries to confess to newlywed Marius that his father-in-law is nothing more than a common thief by showing Marius a portion of the coat from the body from which Valjean was stealing. Of course, the coat belonged to Marius, and Marius discovers that it was Valjean who saved his life. Thénardier's extortion eventually leads to Valjean, Cosette, and Marius reconciling, offering Valjean a final peace before his death.

Joseph says to his brothers who sold him into slavery after rising to power in Egypt, "Even though you intended to do harm to me, God intended it for good, in order to preserve a numerous people, as he is doing today" (Genesis 50:20). Paul proclaims, "We know that all things work together for good for those who love God, who are called according to his purpose" (Romans 8:28). Do we get what we deserve? Thankfully, no. As the great Julia H. Johnston hymn reminds us, "Grace, grace, God's grace, grace that is greater than all our sin."[4]

THE PURE IN HEART

Growing up I had a miniature dachshund named Daisy. Daisy was built like a tiny greyhound. She had a small waist and legs that were long for a dachshund breed. She was so fast that she would catch unassuming squirrels who dared to traverse "her" backyard. The thing I remember most about her is her selective ferociousness. To those she knew she was kind and loving, but to strangers and other dogs she made her presence known. It didn't matter that she stood as tall as my mid-calf. She was always watching, always on guard, and always ready to take down a perceived threat.

Gavroche is a scrappy street urchin who exudes a fierce tenacity, resourcefulness, and a kindness that seems completely foreign to the other "misérables." Gavroche is important to the *Les Misérables* story, but he is not as involved in the narrative as our other characters. Although he is a thief, he steals neither out of spite nor for his own gain. He is aggressive but lovable, tenacious but tenderhearted. His inclusion in *Les Misérables* breaks the stereotype either that the poor are deserving of their fate or that hardship has offered a callousness that makes kindness and generosity strangers.

The musical introduces Gavroche with a lighthearted and bouncy comical number that offers a breath of fresh air after a heavy song showing the terrible poverty in Paris. He warns anyone with ears not to discount those small in stature, with an almost "David vs. Goliath" bravado. Interestingly the music has a purposeful connection to Thénardier's "Master of the House." Both songs are bouncy, but in different ways. Thénardier's song bounces with an ironic triumph, revealing that he is a sham. Gavroche's solo, "Little People," bounces with confidence and frivolity. I love that the two songs offer a nod to one another. Even though it isn't mentioned in the musical, Thénardier is Gavroche's father. It's a subtle connection, but Thénardier and Gavroche are also relative strangers to each other. The music is simply masterful at telling their story.

Gavroche reminds us that looks can be deceiving, but in a different way than we've discussed before. Thénardier initially seems to be a charming war hero who projects hospitality and kindness, but he is a wolf in sheep's clothing. Gavroche seems to be nothing more than a forgotten child of the streets, but he is a symbol of hope in a despondent world. Could it be that even a thief can reveal the grace of God? Does a thief have a role to play in God's story?

Sam Wells tells a poignant story in *Improvisation: The Drama of Christian Ethics*.[5] He talks about a priest who would hire former convicts in his woodworking shop in order to give them a life skill to use as they reenter society. The furniture that these former criminals would make would be donated to those in need around the church. One day he noticed that a woman who lived near the church had no furniture in her one-room apartment, so the men in the shop got to work. After they had built simple bedroom furniture, they loaded the items together and delivered them to her home.

When they arrived, they noticed that no one was home and the doors were locked. The priest invited one of the men, who had been arrested for breaking and entering, to break into the woman's home. After all, the thief was more than qualified to find a way into her home. He opened the door, and they delivered the furniture. As they were leaving, the woman came home. Initially startled at the scene, she quickly realized what the priest had done. She began to cry for the kindness she had received. The priest noticed that the thief was also crying, so he asked why he was troubled. The thief replied, "I've never made someone happy before."

Have you ever been told that there's nothing you can offer? Do you think your past negates any future good that you can offer? Even the thief has a role to play in God's unfolding, graceful drama. It's like the time we started a youth praise band when I was serving as a youth director in Baton Rouge. I invited anyone who wanted to join us to gather in the Wesley Foundation sanctuary for a jam session. We had four singers, drummer, guitarist, bass guitarist, and a tuba player. I wasn't sure how this was going to work, but telling a young person that they weren't needed was not something we were going to do.

We played our first song, "Lord, I Lift Your Name on High." The guitars tuned up, the drummer made sure that his sticks were working as all drummers seem to feel the need to do, and the tuba player warmed up his instrument. We began with the first line, which started better than I had hoped, until the tuba chimed in with a "whomp, whomp, whomp, whomp" following the "sol, la, ti, do" of the major scale. I almost couldn't contain my laughter. He was playing his heart out, but musically, it wasn't working. Thankfully he recognized that it wasn't working too. At some point during the rehearsal there was feedback from one of the microphones, but everyone was busy singing or playing. The young man, who had dejectedly put his tuba down earlier, went behind the sound board and stopped the feedback. In a moment of providence or fate, he had found the role he was called to play.

Looks can certainly be deceiving. Sometimes we think the thief and the tuba player have no role to play until they are invited to sit at the table. Gavroche has a role to play, outside of being a symbol of hope, but it isn't obvious when he enters the story. Gavroche joins the ranks when the students gather at the barricades to rise up against the government in 1832. Gavroche is the one who reveals that Javert is a spy among their ranks. In this way, he is a symbol of truth. He can see beyond disguise and deception. When the revolutionary students are running out of ammunition, Gavroche goes beyond the barricades to collect additional munitions from soldiers who have died, but before he returns to his post, he is shot and dies. It seems that the death of an innocent child wakes them up from their slumber, and they remember the reason why they had come to the barricade. When the death of innocent children no longer stirs our souls to action, it necessitates divine intervention to wake us up. Every time there is a school shooting, I feel defeated even before climbing into the pulpit. It seems that no matter how eloquent or poignant the sermon, it only causes division. Shouldn't the violence speak for itself? There is still so much work to be done.

OFFERING YOURSELF

I am not the tidiest person you've ever met. At least, I hope I'm not. I would like to say that I have a junk drawer near the telephone in the kitchen, but I have several junk drawers. For me, life is too short to organize, label, and strategically pack away items so that they can easily be found when needed later. What's the fun in not having a mild panic attack when you need an important document that you were sure was in the pile of papers at the end of your desk? I feel quite comfortable with improvising in the midst of mildly organized chaos, but I realized early in ministry that when working with others, my "life is too short to organize" attitude is exhausting.

I remember in my first year of being a youth director, I traveled with our youth choir on tour as part of the sound tech team. While on tour everything had to be just so. There was a very specific way the truck had to be loaded and unloaded, our audio setup had to be completed at a precise time, and everything had its place. At the end of the tour I had forgotten the choir director's desire for organization. Things had to be placed in storage in a different way than they had been loaded on the truck, and rather than devise a new "Tetris" configuration, I simply threw items in boxes and tossed them into storage. Life is just too short to label storage items. Things were fine for about ten months until we started tech rehearsal for the next show. When it was time to set up the sound and lights, I went into the storage room and brought all of the equipment down. I will never forget the choir director's face when she saw that the extension cords (some were specific to the lights and others to the soundboard) were tangled together like a hairball of a very large and mangy animal. So, instead of setting up our equipment in time for our first tech rehearsal, I spent most of the rehearsal meticulously untangling extension cords and microphone cables. My impatience with order changed our rehearsal schedule, and I was lovingly but appropriately shamed into never doing it again.

Lent is a time of unraveling for all of the right reasons. I would love to admit that I'm always ready when our forty days of preparation for Christ's resurrection makes its annual return, but more often than not, I look at the closet of my life and realize that I've simply been packing things away to be sorted out later. The day after Ash Wednesday feels very much like that frightful day I spent unraveling cords and cables. Adopting new spiritual practices helps us slowly and intentionally tackle the chaos that we've created. Although it is difficult and often frustrating work, when I take the time to order what needs to be, I feel ready to proclaim, "Christ is risen!" come Resurrection Sunday.

The character Eponine experiences a redemptive unraveling of sorts. Being the oldest of the Thénardiers' children, she was pampered and in want of nothing as a child. She followed her parents' example in treating Cosette with hatred and scorn. When the Thénardiers eventually go bankrupt, Eponine finds herself becoming the "misérable" that she was taught to hate. Much like Cosette, we hear little about Eponine until she reenters the story as a young woman. She is living in Paris and has joined the ranks of the "misérables" who find life to be a daily struggle. Also like Cosette, she has fallen in love with Marius, who lives in the adjacent room to their meager apartment. Cosette and Eponine are indelibly linked, and their characters have experienced a role reversal of sorts. For Eponine, this is more than a "riches to rags" kind of story. Although she has gone from pampered to pauper, her spirit has grown with a richness of selflessness and grace.

John chapter 9 records a role reversal of sorts. The chapter begins when Jesus sees a man who had been blind from birth, and the disciples ask him whether it was his sin or his parents' sin that caused his blindness. Jesus says, "Neither this man nor his parents sinned; he was born blind so that God's works might be revealed in him" (John 9:3). This story is already convicting. How quickly the disciples assumed this man's status as a beggar was the result of sin. Too often poverty is stigmatized as the result of personal choice instead of a symptom of systemic failure. Of course our actions have consequences, but to broadly paint those of a lower economic status as deficient is simply a means of making yourself feel better about your current state. It's like the publican who prayed, "God, I thank you that I am not like other people: thieves, rogues, adulterers, or even like this tax collector" (Luke 18:11).

Jesus spat on the ground to make mud, rubbed the mud in the man's eyes, and then commanded him to go wash in the pool of Siloam. When the man receives his sight, people begin to ask who restored his sight. Of course, the man doesn't know because he was unable to see Jesus. The Pharisees begin to question the man because they simply cannot believe that a blind beggar could have had such an experience. Jesus' healing not only restores his sight, but also restores his dignity and identity. Notice how the blind man's identity is beginning to change. In verse 13 the man is "the man formerly been blind." Now in verse 18 he is "the man who had received his sight." Yes, Jesus healed his eyes, but he is also healing the eyes of those around the man. But here is an interesting thing. Throughout this story the man who regains his sight begins to grow in his understanding of Christ, while the Pharisees become increasingly blind. Those who have been oppressed are being filled with a deep and abiding presence and understanding of Christ while the oppressors are becoming increasingly more shallow and blind. Eventually the blind man begins to teach the Pharisees about who Jesus is; finally he sees Jesus and professes his faith.

Eponine's role reversal with Cosette is both similar to and different from what we see happening in John 9. It is true that Eponine and Cosette trade economic places, but Eponine grows with a compassion that Cosette simply doesn't express. It's not that Cosette is cruel or unkind, but her affluence leaves her apathetic. Although Eponine loves Marius, she knows that he loves Cosette, which is beautifully expressed in the musical number "On My Own." In Hugo's story, as with many other characters, Eponine is not as self-less as the musical presents her. In the book Eponine hides import-ant information in the hope that Marius and Cosette will eventually part. Nevertheless, Eponine's love for Marius leads her to make the ultimate sacrifice. When Marius is at the barricade, he finds him-self in the crosshairs of a soldier's musket. Eponine shields Marius from the bullet and loses her life. Although she had hoped that they would die together, she did not hesitate to step in the way of a bullet.

Poverty is a fascinating character in Hugo's story. In Fantine's story we can see how poverty has the power to destroy the naïve. Thénardier's story reveals that poverty can be a perpetual bedfel-low that propagates selfishness and greed. Gavroche shows us that sometimes those of lesser means are the most generous of us all. And Eponine displays how circumstance can sometimes offer a growth that we thought impossible. But then again, what might the world look like when this great human invention of poverty is no longer with us? As inspiring as Eponine's story may be, how much more inspiring would it be for poverty to have been defeated at the barricade?

4

THE GIFT OF LOVE:
THE STORY OF MARIUS
AND COSETTE

"Love is the folly of men and the wisdom of God."[1]

Any great epic story like *Les Misérables* will inevitably contain an epic love story. While the surrounding events are dark, the love that grows between Marius and Cosette brings light, hope, and motivation to the story. As Christians, our motivation is love. Love of God brings love of neighbor, and that love of neighbor deepens our love of God. Marius and Cosette share one of the few happy endings this story has to offer. Is their marriage Victor Hugo's way of saying that goodness wins out in the end?

COSETTE

Teaching Bible study is one of my favorite things to do. I think I've taught all of the studies within the Disciple Bible Study series, though I have to say that the third installment, "Remember Who You Are," was not my favorite. Early in the year you study the prophets of the Hebrew Scriptures, and several lessons in it feel like the Jewish Temple gets destroyed week after week for several weeks in a row. It's a difficult read, and maybe it's supposed to be. Since I had taught the class before, one year I let the class know to stick with the reading. It's a heavy read to hear about exile and destruction several weeks in a row, but ultimately this story is one that ends well. "Remember Who You Are" is appropriately named. Exile is part of God's story, and though it is difficult, God was still able to offer good in the midst of it.

Cosette's story is one that ends well, though initially it is difficult to read. Cosette is Fantine's daughter, whom she leaves in the care of the Thénardiers. Fantine trusts the Thénardiers because of their charm and seemingly stable home life. Unfortunately, it isn't long before Cosette is harshly treated, abused, and neglected at the expense of the Thénardiers' other children. The musical introduces Cosette, though impoverished and mistreated, with a glimmer of hope. It seems the authors and composers wanted the audience to stick around, just like my "Remember Who You Are" Bible study.

Cosette sings about a dream she has had of her mother who offers her solace and peace. The fact that Cosette is still able to dream is what offers the hope. It seems that dreams and hope go together. Joseph dreamed that his brothers would one day bow down to him (Genesis 37:7). Although Joseph could have been more tactful about the way he shared his dreams with his brothers, this dream was certainly something he could hold on to when he was tossed into a pit, sold into slavery, and jailed in Egypt. Another Joseph, Mary's husband, had a dream not to dismiss his wife before Jesus was born. A dream also told him to flee and seek refuge from Herod after Jesus was born. When the Holy Spirit was poured out upon the disciples, Peter says to the crowd, "In the last days it will be, God declares, that I will pour out my Spirit upon all flesh, and your sons and your daughters shall prophesy, and your young men shall see visions, and your old men shall dream dreams" (Acts 2:17). Hope and dreams go hand in hand, which is why we should be concerned when we've lost the ability to dream. It's difficult to find hope when you can't imagine a tomorrow. Thankfully, against her present circumstance, Cosette is still dreaming, which means there is hope for her yet.

On Christmas Eve, the Thénardiers send Cosette out into the cold to fetch water. On her journey she meets Jean Valjean, who has recently left his post as the Mayor of Montreuil. Valjean is surprised that he has found Fantine's daughter with such ease, recognizing that providence must be at work. He helps her carry the water back to the inn, and upon arriving at the inn, he can see how the young girl has been mistreated. After seeking lodging for the night, Valjean offers the Thénardiers 1,500 francs to part with Cosette. After trying to embezzle him for additional funds, the Thénardiers eventually agree to offer Cosette to this strange visitor. It is not a coincidence that this encounter happens on Christmas Eve. For Cosette, Valjean is a kind of Saint Nicholas. Cosette's "saving" from the Thénardiers and her new life with Valjean is a subtle nod to the Christmas miracle of Christ's birth, a miracle that will change the course of both of their lives.

Have you ever hoped for a miracle? Our church staff is walking through *Eight Virtues of Rapidly Growing Churches*, and I love how the authors Matt Miofsky and Jason Byassee begin their book with an honest reflection about miracles. "After all, we cannot manufacture miracles. We can pray, sure. We can hope. But we can't *make* miracles happen. If church growth is dependent on the surprising, miracle-producing work of the Holy Spirit, then that leaves us pretty helpless. Or so we might think."[2] Miofsky and Byassee recommend neither some quick fixes nor best practices as if there is a magic pill that leads to church growth; rather they recommend prayer, a healthy expectation of God's interjection in the world, and the courage to follow where God is leading. It seems that Cosette's dreams about a heavenly castle on a cloud are prayers that she offers in her own childlike and innocent way. Valjean's tenacity to seek out Fantine's child and pledge to raise her as his own is an answer to this dream. In other words, we are seeing a miracle in Valjean and Cosette's meeting. What fills your prayers? What miracles are you expecting from a God that relentlessly seeks for us?

Here the musical skips ahead to when Cosette is a teenager and living with Valjean on Rue Plumet. In Hugo's story, Valjean and Cosette take up residence in a convent in order to hide from Javert's pursuit. Here they live in relative safety and peace, until Cosette matures and feels stifled and imprisoned. She wants to experience the outside world, which fills Valjean with fear and dread. It is true that they are safe within the convent, but it is a safety that also feels like imprisonment.

This fear and dread is something with which I am quite familiar. Being the father of four children, I always try to find a balance between offering them freedom to make their own decisions while also offering safety, guidance, and protection. My children are relatively young, so I rarely worry about where they are and whom they are with, but this balance is becoming more difficult with the pervasiveness of technology. It is so very interesting that I will live most of my Christian life in a context with which Jesus was unfamiliar. There are days that I wish Jesus had written a "Parent's Guide to Raising Children." It would be helpful for Jesus to have offered a clear picture of what Christian parenthood was all about. On the other hand, if I read such a manual, I wonder how accomplished I would be in following it.

Valjean does his best to keep Cosette safe, but he also hasn't revealed to her why they need to hide. She just assumes that he is being overly protective. He eventually concedes to Cosette's constant request for freedom, and they slowly begin to venture outside the walls of the convent. Cosette has become a beautiful but naïve young woman. Thankfully, the abuse she received at such a young age seems relatively forgotten, for she looks at the world with optimistic fervor. It could be that her zealous optimism is a means of burying the pain of her childhood, but it's hard to say. She seems genuine, hopeful, and delightful; but it isn't long before this newfound freedom offers new challenges to Valjean and Cosette. These new challenges do not come from Javert, the police, or Thénardier, but from a source Valjean had not expected—love.

MARIUS

In the initial chapters of his fantastic book *The Irrational Jesus*, Ken Evers-Hood talks about how we are often unaware of the ways we are influenced by the outside world. We are not nearly as rational and in control of our decisions as we think we are. In chapter 2, he details Dan Ariely's "Matrix Study," in which a group of students was asked to complete a series of math problems for which they were paid for each correct answer. One group had to turn in their work to be graded by one of the facilitators. The other group was given the opportunity to grade their own paper and destroy their test (which wasn't actually destroyed). Can you guess which group scored higher? It is not surprising to know that the group who self-scored ended up getting more answers correct.

What's more interesting in this experiment was the way in which the different groups were conditioned prior to taking the test. Outside of the control group, one group was asked to write down ten books that they had read from high school. The other group was asked to write down as many of the Ten Commandments that they could remember. Interestingly, the group that wrote down the Ten Commandments prior to taking the test tended to self-score more honestly—"In other studies Dan has shown that this religious priming promotes integrity, at least in the short term, as does having people sign honor codes."[3] This also may not be a surprise to you, but this reveals the importance of theological education as well as just how susceptible we are to suggestion and influence.

Marius is very susceptible to the direction the wind is blowing. He is idealistic and passionate and represents the romanticism of mid-nineteenth-century aristocracy. In the musical, Marius's character seems to be a means to an end. It's as if the librettists needed a love story to make the musical complete, and they added Marius as Cosette's love interest as an afterthought. With any medium outside of an original work, decisions have to be made in what to include and what to leave on the cutting room floor. On the one hand I am thankful that the musical isn't a week long in an attempt to include all of the narrative points Hugo is trying to make. On the other hand the musical misses an opportunity to dive into why Marius matters in the story.

Marius is the grandson of M. Gillenormand, a gruff throwback to the enlightenment who detested Napoleon and anything outside the regal authority of the monarchy. M. Gillenormand had two daughters, the younger of whom was Marius's mother. She was the very definition of a romantic. She appreciated poetry, loved nature, and dreamed of living a comfortable life in the arms of her one true love, which means she often received her father's scorn of rationalism and order. Marius's father, Georges Pontmercy, wasn't as romantic as his mother, but he was even more disparaged and vilified by Marius's grandfather because he was a colonel and a member of Napoleon's Legion of Honor. Marius's mother died when Marius was young, so M. Gillenormand assumed guardianship of the young boy and forbade him to ever see his father. He would tell Marius that his father was a traitor and a crook, and keeping them apart was best for both of them.

This constant disparaging of his father conditioned Marius into being a supporter of the crown, and all the politics along with it. As an adolescent he was a loud and boisterous supporter of the monarchy, which put him at odds with several of his classmates. Marius's father is not nearly the bandit that he assumes him to be. Colonel Pontmercy would often sneak into Paris on Sundays and watch over his son at a distance during mass at Saint-Sulpice Church. When the colonel was near death, Marius grudgingly goes to see him. Unfortunately, he dies before Marius arrives, leaving only a letter behind. The letter details his father's accomplishments which read—

> The Emperor named me baron on the battlefield of Waterloo. Since the Restoration questions the title I won with my blood, my son will take it and bear it. . . . At the same battle of Waterloo, a sergeant saved my life. The man is called Thénardier. . . . If my son meets him he will be as helpful as he can.[4]

Discovering the truth about his father sends Marius into a whirlwind. He tries to learn as much about his father as he can, which leads to a complete change in his worldview. He becomes a staunch supporter of the Empire, rejects the monarchy, and begins to feel the winds of change his classmates have been trumpeting.

It is easy to see how Marius can now be appalled by everything his grandfather supported. Have you ever discovered something that made you rethink everything? I remember the first time I recognized that Jesus had wounds to show Thomas after the Resurrection (John 20). I always had a picture in my head that after the Resurrection Jesus' body was glowing and perfect, hardly resembling his previous body. It makes sense. Jesus isn't recognized on the road to Emmaus. The disciples aren't really sure it is Jesus on the lakeshore. But then we have this fantastic story of the resurrected Christ showing his wounds to Thomas. It was at that moment that I realized that the healing of our wounds is what defines us. Being wounded is not our identity. Forgetting our wounds does little to erase them. What truly defines who we are as Christians is how our wounds are healed.

On the one hand I can appreciate Marius's drastic transformation, but this is not the last time that Marius will radically change his devotions. Enjolras convinces Marius to join a group of his friends who are preparing to take up arms against the monarchy and help the oppressed. Once again Marius changes his allegiance. In a short time he has moved from Monarchist to Imperialist to Republican revolutionary. Hugo seems to want us to know how fickle we can be. Regardless if monarchy or republic is the best form of governance, Marius seems to be conditioned to accept the latest philosophy he hears.

In what ways have you been conditioned to accept the teachings you've been offered? Are you even aware that conditioning is happening at all? Our political leanings have much less to do with how we think government should work and more to do with the people who surround us. If the people we love and trust vote with a particular party, we are much more likely to vote with the same party. The same holds true for other segregations like denominational affiliation. I would love to say that all Methodists are Methodist because of John Wesley's understanding of prevenient, justifying, and sanctifying grace, but more often than not, they feel connected to the people who are sitting in the pews with them. Joining a church because of the people isn't a bad thing, though we must always be aware that the story we've been given isn't the only story told.

Finding Each Other

Marius leaves his aristocratic life behind with only thirty francs in his pocket after a confrontation with his grandfather. There is a great generational divide between Marius and his grandfather. M. Gillenormand is stuck in his eighteenth-century worldview while Marius sets out to make his own way in a new world. This divide seems to be as old as time itself. I remember my mother talking about how she and her mother got into arguments about how radical the Beatles were, and that good girls wouldn't listen to these crazy mop-topped teens. These confrontations were not unlike the conversations I would have with my mother when blaring 311 from my Bob Marley and Beastie Boy stickered car. I almost shudder at the thought of the conversations I'll have with my kids one day.

Marius starts off on his own, and things do not go well at first. Do you know or remember those first few steps out on your own? I remember my first night away when I went off to college. At first, I felt an amazing sense of freedom and excitement, but it wasn't long before I called my parents, making sure that they had a safe journey home just to hear their voices. It's scary to set out on your own. Can you imagine being like Abram and God calling you to leave your family behind to go to a place that God will later reveal?

Now the LORD said to Abram, "Go from your country and your kindred and your father's house to the land that I will show you. I will make of you a great nation, and I will bless you, and make your name great, so that you will be a blessing. I will bless those who bless you, and the one who curses you I will curse; and in you all the families of the earth shall be blessed." (Genesis 12:1-3)

God offers Abram a great promise, yet the Lord doesn't offer as many specifics as maybe you or I would like. As an elder in The United Methodist Church, I always keep my phone nearby when I know that the bishop's cabinet is meeting at the turn of the calendar year. Elders itinerate, which means we serve where the bishop sends us. As with anything, the itinerant system has its blessings and growing edges. One thing I love about being sent to new places with new faces is that having a new pastor constantly reminds us that the work of the church is about Christ and not about a pastor's gifts (or lack thereof). If I received a call from my district superintendent telling me that my next appointment was a growing community of faith where I will be a blessing for generations to come, but she didn't tell me where I was going, I might be hesitant to pack up the family and hit the road. Being sent to a fruitful place is certainly enough, but it would be nice to know what to put into your GPS.

Our calling might not be as dramatic as Abram's, but God does call us all the time to move forward into an uncertain future. Maybe you are starting a new job, or you have become a first-time parent, or maybe soon you'll be going to college away from home. Every day is full of uncertainties, which is why we must rely on the Holy Spirit. Before Jesus began his ministry, the Spirit "drove him out into the wilderness. He was in the wilderness forty days, tempted by Satan" (Mark 1:12-13). There is a slight difference between Mark and Matthew's Gospel as to why Jesus was sent away. Mark's Gospel offers no background information or reasoning. Verse 12 only tells us that the Spirit drove Jesus into the wilderness. Matthew's Gospel softens the language and offers just a hint more to the story. Matthew records, "Then Jesus was led up by the Spirit into the wilderness to be tempted by the devil"

(Matthew 4:1). Matthew offers a reason as to why the Spirit was leading Jesus. There is a point and a purpose to such curious travel plans. Mark leaves us guessing for a moment. Although only a period and a space separate verses 12 and 13, I would imagine that the time between going to the wilderness and understanding why you are there felt like forty days in and of itself. Whether or not we know why God is calling us to where God is leading, thankfully the only thing we need to know is that God will be there.

So, Marius sets out not knowing what the future will bring. Although he is alone, he isn't lonely. He often takes walks in the Luxembourg Gardens relatively indifferent to the passersby. He notices an older gentleman with a younger girl, but initially doesn't pay them any mind. About six months later, he notices Cosette, who is now a young woman, and he is spellbound. Marius's sudden infatuation with Cosette is one of the few places where the musical and the book agree. Cosette's beauty seems to consume him, but this also is true to Marius's character. As a romantic, he dives deep into the emotional well with every novelty. From Monarchist to Imperialist to Republican to lover, and this is not the last time that his passion will shift.

Sometimes when we think about Scripture, we don't think about romantic love. The "Song of Solomon" is an entire book devoted to the kind of desire Marius is feeling for Cosette.

> *As an apple tree among the trees of the wood,*
> *   so is my beloved among young men.*
> *With great delight I sat in his shadow,*
> *   and his fruit was sweet to my taste.*
> *He brought me to the banqueting house,*
> *   and his intention toward me was love.*
> *Sustain me with raisins,*
> *   refresh me with apples;*
> *   for I am faint with love. (Song of Solomon 2:3-5)*

Marius is certainly "faint with love," but most often when Scripture talks about love it means "loyalty," "devotion," or "kindness." The Hebrew word *khesed*, meaning love/loyalty, appears about 250 times in the Old Testament.[5] For example, when the Lord passed before Moses on Mount Sinai we read, "The Lord, the Lord, / a God merciful and gracious, / slow to anger, / and abounding in steadfast love (*khesed*) and faithfulness, / keeping steadfast love (*khesed*) for the thousandth generation" (Exodus 34:6-7a).

This kind of love isn't necessarily what Marius is feeling. The love most mentioned throughout Scripture is a steadfastness that remains through the ebbing of desire and indifference. I think Danish theologian Søren Kierkegaard said it best—"Passion enflames, worldly sagacity cools, but neither this heat nor this cold, nor the combination of this heat and this cold is the pure air of the eternal."[6] The love of God is a love that remains steadfast whether we support the crown or the republic. You certainly cannot fault Marius for being head over heels in love with Cosette, but Marius is a cautionary tale of what happens when our emotions go unchecked, which we will soon see.

LOVE AND TRUTH

I think my ten-year-old daughter Annaleigh will one day find a lucrative career in writing Hallmark cards. She is kind, compassionate, and empathetic. No matter the occasion, she is quick to put pen to paper to tell people how important, talented, or special they are. This year for Father's Day she made me a card saying:

> Father's Day is one of my favorite holidays. It's the one day of the year to appreciate all the work my dad has done. All the rain you walked through for us, all the writing you've written for us, and all the work you've done for us. The list goes on

through eternity and life itself, but I only have one piece of paper. In a whole crowd of people at a Dave Matthews concert, you will always stand out (in a great wonderful way).

This is just one of the many letters my sweet daughter has written. My favorite thing about her writing is that she often uses phrases like, "eternity and life itself." Last year she wrote, "You are like a beautiful magnolia tree with leaves of mistakes falling behind you. And you are like water from the roots. You shoot up higher and higher until you reach the top." See what I mean? Writing letters is certainly her love language, and I hope her desire to make people feel special is something that never goes away.

Marius and Cosette write letters back and forth to one another expressing their love. It isn't long before Valjean discovers their relationship, and out of fear of losing the one person he had ever grown to love, he plans to take Cosette away to England. Marius is devastated that Cosette is leaving, which is why he finally joins his comrades at the barricades. Marius brings an almost reckless bravery to the uprising. He is fearless because he feels without Cosette there is nothing for which to live. Cosette, too, is heartbroken. Marius has left Cosette a note saying that if he dies at the barricade, he will die loving her. When Valjean discovers that Marius has joined the revolutionary ranks, Valjean journeys to meet him, though his intentions are unclear. Here, the recent Masterpiece adaptation of *Les Misérables* really shines. You can see the ambiguity on Valjean's face. Is he going to the barricade to save Marius for the sake of Cosette? Is he going to the barricade to make sure Marius never returns? This is a far cry from the heroic Valjean in the musical during the epic song "One Day More."

The barricades in Hugo's story represent more than a revolutionary tactic. A barricade is a roadblock, something that gets in the way. On the surface the barricade is meant to be a symbol of turning the government upside down, but it seems that it's also upending the characters who seek its shelter. Grantaire, one of Enjolras's friends who initially is passionate about fighting for the people, ends up in a fearful and drunken stupor when the fighting begins. Marius isn't fighting to bring about a new world like Enjolras; rather he's given up on the world altogether. Javert gives up his integrity to become a spy behind the wall. Valjean takes up arms in order to protect his own happiness and solitude. At the barricades everything is upside down.

It's like when Jesus goes to the land of the Gerasenes in Luke chapter 8. The story begins with, "Then they arrived at the country of the Gerasenes, which is opposite Galilee" (Luke 8:26). This land (and this story) is very opposite Galilee indeed. There Jesus meets a demoniac who knows who he is, when the disciples are still confused—"Who then is this, that he commands even the winds and the water, and they obey him" (Luke 8:25). The Gerasene economy is based on raising swine, which would make a Jew unclean. After Jesus heals the man, the town begs Jesus to leave them alone. And when the man requests to follow Jesus, Jesus tells him to go home. This story is so very opposite Galilee indeed.

Have you ever had an experience when everything just seemed upside down? Hurricane Katrina changed just about everything in the New Orleans area in the late summer of 2005. Even though I was living in North Carolina at the time, the rest of my family took the full brunt of the storm. My sister, who had a one-month-old premature child who needed an apnea machine to monitor her heart rate, had to evacuate. They didn't get back into their home until a year and a half later. My parents evacuated to a different place than my sister. No one could get in touch with anyone else because of damaged cell towers. My mother remembers that when they did get back in town to check on their home, there were armed guards at the local Walmart. Things just didn't seem real.

Everything seems upside down at the barricades. The revolutionaries initially gather with, "No one has greater love than this, to lay down one's life for one's friends" (John 15:13) ringing in their ears, but even this is turned on its head. Very few at the barricades are fighting for the republic. Most are fighting only for themselves, but then the dynamic changes. The joyful and fearless Gavroche is gunned down while gathering munitions from the dead National Guardsmen. His death seems to shake the revolutionaries from their selfish daze. Marius goes beyond the barricade to retrieve his body, signaling that there is something worth fighting for. Valjean fortifies the barricade, hinting that his wrestling over whether or not to save Marius has subsided. It seems that the loss of innocence reignited their passion. "Sleeper, awake! / Rise from the dead, / and Christ will shine on you" (Ephesians 5:14), the author of Ephesians writes. Gavroche laying down his life for his friends snaps them back to where they need to be.

Although the revolutionaries have a newfound passion, the National Guard brings their uprising to a quick and tragic end. Near the end of the fighting Valjean drags a critically wounded Marius through the Paris sewers to safety. Valjean has resigned himself to saving Marius even if it costs him everything. Eventually Marius is delivered home to M. Gillenormand, and he makes a full recovery. Valjean allows Cosette to marry Marius even though he is filled with a great sadness. If you have ever been the parent of a bride or groom, you understand the strange combination of a painful joy when you see the new couple walking down the aisle hand in hand. There is joy that two people have found each other, but there is a sadness in knowing that nothing will ever be the same. In addition to saying goodbye to Cosette, Valjean feels compelled to finally admit his true identity. It is indeed a mournful joy. It's kind of like receiving a card that says, "You are like a beautiful magnolia tree with leaves of mistakes falling behind you, and you are like water from the roots. You shoot up higher and higher until you reach the top."

THE GREATEST OF THESE IS LOVE

Marius is the very definition of a French Romantic. As I've said, he moves to extremes with a deep passion as if his latest experience is the truth. We do the same thing throughout our life, though maybe not to the extreme of a young romantic. I remember when I was in high school I had everything figured out (with the exception of advanced math). My parents thought they were so smart with their rules and curfews and financial planning. Almost like magic my parents became much smarter when my wife and I started having children. I'm not sure how to explain their sudden giftedness, but I am thankful that they finally were blessed with wisdom when I needed it.

Of course it was I and not them who changed. Like Marius, I have had my fair share of convictions overturned and philosophies proven false. It's like being convinced that the sun is setting until realizing that the earth is turning. It's not an accident that Marius and Cosette's marriage is near the end of our story. This naïve ingénue and fickle romantic finding each other and starting a new life together is where Hugo wants to leave us. It is a symbol of hope and stability for a world that seems perilous and fragile, but the story isn't quite finished for these two lovers.

Marius and Cosette's relationship brings about a dance between truth and reconciliation. It takes six months for Marius to fully recover from his injury, and during this time M. Gillenormand never leaves his side. The old curmudgeon set to send Marius away couldn't bear the thought of losing his heir. Sometimes our squabbles and disagreements seem so small when placed into perspective with the rest of our journey. I do not contend that God causes pain, illness, or grief, but these life-changing events help us see how often we are consumed with things that may not ultimately matter. It's like when the father welcomes home the prodigal in Luke 15. We aren't told why the young man wanted his inheritance, or why he was bent on leaving his home. What we do know is that while he was still far off his father ran out to meet him, and in that moment the young man's presence was the only thing that mattered.

When Marius recovers, his grandfather is overjoyed, though Marius is consumed with thoughts of Cosette. Marius defiantly asks his grandfather's permission to marry Cosette, and to Marius's amazement, his grandfather agrees. This becomes a powerful moment of reconciliation for the two of them. Marius even calls M. Gillenormand "Father," and the two never again speak of their different political affinities.

After Marius and Cosette are married, Valjean arranges a meeting with Marius to confess his true identity. He explains that he is nothing more than a thief and criminal, never mentioning the good that he has done, including saving Marius's life. Valjean's confession repulses Marius, causing him at first to forbid Valjean from ever visiting. Again, Marius, without questioning, prodding, or investigating, accepts the truth of what he's heard. Valjean's heart is broken. He feels that this is divine retribution for his crimes, so he accepts his banishment, disappears into solitude, and slowly begins to lose his health.

Through a chance encounter with Thénardier, Marius discovers that it was Valjean who saved his life, and again the pendulum swings in the other direction for this young romantic. Finally, the full truth of Valjean is unveiled, and Marius, Cosette, and Valjean are reconciled—filling Valjean's final moments with joy and happiness.

Cosette and Marius's marriage is more than a love story that ends well. Their union brings about reconciliation, joy, and hope to an otherwise difficult story. Marriage is an outward and visible way of recognizing an inward and spiritual grace revealing how Christ is united to the church. Hugo seems to suggest that the romantic and the ingénue receiving wisdom and security from the previous generation in order to build a hopeful future is his picture of what the world should be. His metaphor is less about marriage than it is about the hope of reconciliation between the old and the new, and the stability necessary to build a better world.

What am I to say about love? Paul in his letter to the Corinthian church seems to be having a difficult time nailing down exactly what love is. It's almost like we are overhearing Paul ramble trying to find the right words. He says that love is patient and kind. Love is not envious or boastful or arrogant or rude. It bears and believes all things. It's like Paul is trying to say that love is the only thing that really exists, and in this way, "God is love" (1 John 4:8) rings true.

Love is the one thing we can experience that defies time or circumstance. Love is the beginning and the ending of God's story, from Creation to Resurrection to re-creation. Too often we like to start God's story with Genesis 3 (God's punishment for eating the fruit of the tree of the knowledge of good and evil) and end it with Revelation 20 (death and judgment), but if you extend the story on either side you will see that our story is one of love.

"No one has greater love than this, to lay down one's life for one's friends" (John 15:13). This is God's story in the person of Jesus. Jesus offered his life through teaching and healings, always on the move to seek out the lost like the Good Shepherd. Jesus offered his life on the cross, revealing God's vulnerable love emptied and on display in a world where influence, wealth, and status are thought to be the only powers. Jesus offered his life to us in the Resurrection, revealing that wounds can be healed, forgiveness is possible, and everything that Jesus taught can be trusted as the truth. We are called to be a living sacrifice, offering our life as stewards of God's love in the world. Marriage is one of God's greatest gifts, offering us the opportunity to practice fidelity, trust, and sacrificial living for the building of a present and future hope. Of course, marriage isn't the only way to become a living sacrifice, but in the context of *Les Misérables* it is abundantly clear that Marius and Cosette's love for each other is the vehicle through which hope is discovered.

Paul writes, "Faith, hope, and love abide, these three; and the greatest of these is love" (1 Corinthians 13:13). Faith is trusting that God will do what God promised to do. Hope is trusting in things not yet seen. Love is certainly the greatest of these because it is the glue that holds faith and hope together. The love story between Marius and Cosette gives us hope. Even in the midst of suffering, violence, misplaced notions of justice, and human-made poverty, love is still at work.

5

BUILDING THE BARRICADE: THE STORY OF *LES AMIS*

"It was like a rising tide complicated by a thousand eddies."[1]

Paris is a powder keg ready to ignite into flames. After Napoleon was defeated and exiled in 1814, leadership fell to two Bourbon kings, Louis XVIII and Charles X, who reigned for the next sixteen years. This period, known as The Restoration, attempted to maintain a peaceful order with a strong monarchy while maintaining public rights won during the French Revolution. When it became obvious that a monarchy with republican ideals was not going to work, the king was overthrown and replaced with a more sympathetic leader, Louis Philippe. The constant upheaval only ignited thoughts of a complete overthrow of the government, which sends the students at St. Denis into a frenzy.

Every revolution needs at least three ingredients—a problem, a solution, and a leader. Regardless if either problem or solution is real or perceived, a revolution is meant to overthrow, overturn, destroy, or upend the way things are. In the case of *Les Misérables*, the "Friends of the ABC" are ready to take up arms against the French monarchy in order to establish a republic that will offer freedom to the oppressed and impoverished. "Friends of the ABC" is actually a play on words. The French pronunciation of ABC sounds like the French word, *abaissé*, which means "oppressed." Their aim is clear, but is it warranted? Is there any guarantee that a republic will be better equipped to bring equity between the wealthy and the poor? Will an uprising backfire and bring even more oppression to the people? Is there a way to bring about justice without picking up arms? Meditating on the events of Jesus' last week in Jerusalem helps us rethink conventional notions of revolution.

FANNING THE FLAMES

Jesus entered Jerusalem on the back of a donkey to announce his messiahship. The crowd that had gathered would have recognized the significance of Jesus on a beast of burden. Zechariah 9:9 says, "Lo, your king comes to you; / triumphant and victorious is he, / humble and riding on a donkey, / on a colt, the foal of a donkey." The crowd is shouting, "Hosanna," which means "Save us!" This triumphant entry would certainly be enough to get the attention of the Roman authority, who would hear the shouts of salvation as a political referendum defying Roman occupation. The Romans aren't wrong to be fearful of an uprising. Taking Jesus' last week as a whole, it seems that the crowd was begging for a political revolution. Near the end of the week when Jesus was arrested and beaten, the crowd's "Hosanna" became "Crucify him." There is little more embarrassing than supporting a seemingly failed revolutionary leader.

The funeral march for General Lamarque in *Les Misérables* is like this beginning of Holy Week. It serves as the spark that ignites the people to build the barricades against the government. On June 5, 1832, the body of General Lamarque, a hero of the Empire and a supporter of the left, is led in procession for burial. The "Friends of the ABC," along with many others, come to the parade armed and ready. Much like the Romans who would send extra military assistance to Jerusalem during the Passover, the Parisian government posted over 24,000 troops in Paris and the surrounding areas. During the tense and emotional gathering, shots are fired and barricades are erected throughout the city.

Maybe one of Jesus' miracles that goes unmentioned is the relative peace that's recorded when Jesus entered Jerusalem. He enters the city as a Messiah King, and he goes to the Temple to drive out the moneychangers. Jesus even raises the stakes when the religious leaders tell him to order his disciples to stop shouting in the streets. Jesus replies, "I tell you, if these were silent, the stones would shout out" (Luke 19:40). This is a prophetic slam against the Pharisees, remembering Habakkuk 2:9-11, which reads,

> "Alas for you who get evil gain for your house,
>   setting your nest on high
>   to be safe from the reach of harm!"
> You have devised shame for your house
>   by cutting off many peoples;
>   you have forfeited your life.
> The very stones will cry out from the wall,
>   and the plaster will respond from the woodwork.

Even though the religious leaders were plotting against Jesus, not a sword is unsheathed. At least, not yet. The students at St. Denis quickly built barricades all over the city. Weapons were gathered, and munitions factories were plundered. The government soldiers held their post, and the city was filled with suspense and dread. Though Scripture isn't explicit, I would imagine the same held true in Jerusalem. We know little about what happened between Jesus' triumphant entry and his Last Supper with the disciples outside of some of Jesus' teachings and Judas meeting with the chief priests. Certainly there were murmurings and conversations about what it all meant.

Have you ever found yourself in a "what does it all mean?" kind of moment? Maybe you saw a breaking news story about military tension, received a call from a loved one with bad news, or were sitting by a hospital bed when difficult results were given. It's hard to do anything other than hold your breath. Once the initial shock subsides, conjecture ensues. In these moments some become experts, thinking they know exactly how something is going to work out. Others run to the poles of optimism or pessimism with their imagination taking the driver's seat. Still others try to ignore the tension, hoping that by looking the other way the tension will disappear.

The disciples didn't know quite how to react to Jesus' Jerusalem entrance either. John's Gospel says, "His disciples did not understand these things at first; but when Jesus was glorified, then they remembered that these things had been written of him and had been done to him" (John 12:16). The disciples seem to wait. Would Jesus give a call to arms? Would Jesus march to Pilate? Was this only the beginning of a sustained resistance against Rome?

Waiting does not come easily to me. When inspiration hits, or someone has an idea for a new ministry or project, I am very quick to jump in and move full steam ahead. Sometimes this is a successful way to be in ministry, but often it is not. Last year we had our first-ever kids drama camp at the church I serve. My mother had organized a drama camp at my home church for years, and I had seen the fruit that drama camp produced. Children gained confidence, parents enjoyed serving at the church one week during the summer, and all felt the Spirit move creating a stage show in five short days. We had tossed the idea around of hosting a drama camp, and I very quickly said "yes!" It didn't take long to realize that I may have moved too quickly. There wasn't any kind of budget for a drama camp. Who was going to run sound and lights? Who was going to teach music? Do we need T-shirts? Should the kids stay for lunch? Would anyone show up? Thankfully drama camp is a story that ends well, but I probably lost a few years of my life in the process. And maybe against reason, we're doing it again this year.

Have you ever moved too quickly without weighing all of the options? Maybe the disciples had been with Jesus long enough to have the discipline to wait, listen, and be attentive to what Jesus might do next. As I wrote in this chapter's introduction, every revolution has three ingredients—a problem, a solution, and a leader. Enjolras is the leader of the 1832 uprising. He is idealistic, confident, and charismatic. He has a clear vision that a republic is needed to bring prosperity to France. He chooses General Lamarque's funeral procession to be the rallying point, but soon after, shots are fired and barricades are built. There isn't much of a plan as to what the uprising is meant to accomplish. There is a mild skirmish, and several lose their lives. It isn't long before the reality of the insurrection begins to set in with the comrades who have joined together. When dusk settles in, they wait. They wait, they ponder, and they sing songs together not knowing what the morning will bring.

Their first night at the barricades is not unlike the disciples' last night with Jesus. They gather to break bread, drink wine, sing songs, and ponder what it all means. Neither group understood the significance of their gathering. For both, it was the last time that all would be present around the table and behind the barricades. It's a sobering thought that at some point we have said "I love you" to someone for the last time. Most of the time we are unaware of these final goodbyes, which means that we should treat every moment as meaningful and precious. None of us has any guarantees. The friends at the barricades had no idea what the morning would bring, the disciples didn't know that Jesus would soon be arrested, and we don't know when we've seen our last sunrise.

WHO SHOULD SIT ON THE THRONE?

A revolution seeks to upend the way things are, and this usually has everything to do with who has power, how they maintain power, and at whose expense. Pilate has the power in Judea during Jesus' ministry. Judea is so unruly during Jesus' lifetime that the normal way of Roman rule no longer applies. Normally, Rome would put in place a puppet king so that they might collect taxes, acquire land and resources, and keep their hands clean of the day-to-day nuisance of ruling. This is what the Empire had in place with Herod the Great. They propped up a puppet and enjoyed the spoils. Not anymore. Pilate is the governor with a hands-on approach to order, so there is no mistake who is in charge, nor is there a mistake as to what really matters: wealth, prestige, and power, and Jesus threatens all three.

John's Gospel presents Jesus' interaction with Pontius Pilate in seven short scenes. In scene one, the Jewish authorities hand Jesus over to Pilate, but they remain outside the governor's home so that they can remain ritually pure for the upcoming Passover meal. This tells us almost all we need to know about the religious ruling class. They are fine with putting an innocent man to death, as long as they can remain ritually pure. The collateral damage of their quest for personal holiness is never weighed or measured or found consequential.

The French elite wouldn't dare mingle with those perceived to be lower than their status. This is why Javert remains on his horse early in the story when Fauchelevent is pinned under his cart in Montreuil, causing M. Madeleine (Valjean) to intervene. Was Javert's apathy a means of setting a trap for the suspected Valjean? Was Javert so concerned with status that even helping to save a life is below him? It's hard to say. How often is Jesus' parable about the good Samaritan played out in our daily lives? Have we ever passed by on the other side of the road? Has our perceived status of self-importance gotten in the way of taking a risk for the good of the gospel?

It's important to note the unique setting in John's Gospel of Jesus' final days. In Matthew, Mark, and Luke, Jesus is handed over after sharing the Passover meal. In John, Jesus is arrested on the day of preparation, the day before the Passover meal. When John the Baptist says that Jesus is the Lamb of God who takes away the sins of the world, he means it. Jesus will be crucified when the lambs are slaughtered at the Temple for the feast. John crafts his story to show us that in this divine drama, Pilate is Pharaoh, Rome is Egypt, and the Jerusalem authorities are a failed version of Moses. In other words, John is reminding us that the story between the powerful and the powerless is an ancient one. We saw it in Egypt. We saw it in Judea. We saw it in nineteenth-century France. How do we see it today? It's easier to talk about oppression of the poor in days gone by, but we've learned little if we aren't able to recognize the similarities in our own time.

In scene two, Pilate asks Jesus if he is a king. Jesus replies that his kingdom is not of this world. Understand that this doesn't mean that Jesus has been relegated to being the leader of a spiritual reality;

rather his kingdom is not rooted in the world that gives rise to Caesar. Jesus' kingdom is not rooted in a peace rooted in fear or violence. Christ's kingdom is not rooted in ruining others to get to the top. My kingdom is not here, Jesus says. Pilate misunderstands and says, "So you are a king?" "You say that I am a king," is the response, because your imagination is so deprived that you have no word to use for someone who has come to proclaim the truth. Pilate responds by asking, "What is truth?" Pilate is not interested in a debate between his understanding of truth and Jesus' proclamation as if they are in a university symposium or debate class. Pilate is asking as if he's hearing the word for the first time. Being a politician in Rome, the word and its meaning are completely foreign to him.

We see this scene play out in the different political discussions that happen in the middle of *Les Misérables*. Was Napoleon's Empire the best way to govern? Is there really a difference between a king and an emperor? Will a republic really solve economic woes, or will having a president hungry for power simply supplant one form of oppression with another? This is where revolutions can be shortsighted. Are we really taking up arms to develop a new form of governance, or are we trading one oppressor for another?

In scene three, the crowd is given a choice between Jesus and Barabbas, a bandit. This choice reveals that sometimes the majority chooses very poorly, and in this case the majority has chosen a bandit and an insurrectionist. They have chosen someone who picks up the sword, and Rome is all too pleased to offer him to the crowd because they know that Barabbas with a sword is a battle they can win and always will win. One who puts down the sword, one who leads a revolution through giving the poor a voice, restoring sight to the blind, one who can heal without asking for a commodity in return, one who can feed the masses without going to the Roman marketplace, one who can lead a revolution of people who have no fear is one who must be stopped at all costs.

You cannot expect something new to emerge if the system remains the same, no matter who has the title of leader. For a brief time I was a consultant with Youth Ministry Architects. A few times a year a lead consultant and I would partner with a local church looking to transform their youth or young adult ministry. One of the missteps faith communities often make when looking to revitalize a ministry is to assume that if they just find the right leader everything will change. Leadership is certainly important to a ministry's success, but even the best leaders will fail when the surrounding system is ill or needs rebuilding. In other words, we look for Superman to fix our problems, but we place him in kryptonite and wonder why change didn't happen. The people choose Barabbas because they've always chosen Barabbas. This is a choice Rome will offer over and over again.

WHEN ONLY BLOODSHED REMAINS

In scene four, Pilate is done with conversation. Only brutality and shame remain. They fashion a crown of thorns and place it upon his head and offer Jesus a purple robe and present him to the crowd. There's no turning back now. Jesus has become a joke. Shaming someone really doesn't matter if the someone being shamed and ridiculed is seen as "less than," or "other." This is how oppressors work. If you present someone as less than, then violence against them feels appropriate, acceptable, or even ordained.

Javert only sees criminals as "other." They are beyond redemption, and they cannot help but be a menace to society. When this is his default picture, we can see why Valjean makes no sense to Javert. Why would Valjean as the Mayor of Montreuil stoop so low to come to Fantine's aid? Why would Valjean admit that he is Prisoner 24601 in Arras? It's Javert's job to convict, not the criminal's job to openly confess. We wonder why we get into the church

THE GRACE OF *LES MISÉRABLES*

squabbles that we do. Divisions both great and small are often rooted in a misrepresentation of the person or people with whom you disagree.

In scene five, Pilate begins to use Jesus as the puppet he has created him to be, dangling him in front of the crowd. "You take him to be crucified. I find nothing wrong with him." This is not a pronouncement of innocence. Seeing Jesus as bloodied, pathetic, and voiceless is exactly how Pilate views the Jewish people. The crowd responds saying that Rome needs to do this because they do not have the authority to put a man to death. Of course this isn't entirely true. The crowd was quick to pick up stones to murder the woman who was caught in adultery. Again, when you treat someone as other, then violence against them seems appropriate, acceptable, or even ordained.

But the crowd does say something that leaves Pilate uneasy in scene six. They say, "He ought to die because he claims to be the Son of God." Pilate, being familiar with the Roman pantheon of gods, becomes nervous. It's one thing if Jesus claims to be a king. But what if Jesus is a god? What if Jesus is a hero like Hercules or Ulysses? Pilate brings Jesus inside to ask him away from the crowd, "Where do you come from?" This is the first answer John's Gospel offers us: "In the beginning was the Word, and the Word was with God, and the Word was God (John 1:1). Jesus is silent, and Pilate is offended. "Don't you understand I have the power here?" Pilate responds. Again, only the powerful have the privilege of being silent when they want to be. For the seemingly powerless, silence is suspicious, rude, or disrespectful. "I have the power here," Pilate wants Jesus to hear. Jesus responds saying that any power he enjoys has been given to him by someone more powerful than he, and the one offering power is not Caesar.

Pilate is now very afraid. In this scene seven, power has completely reversed. Pilate wants to release Jesus, but in so doing the crowd would revolt, and Pilate would be out of a job for not controlling the people. Pilate has been revealed to be a sham. Pilate is now powerless. There's only one thing he can do. He dangles Jesus before the crowd again saying, Shall I crucify your king? Understand this is no longer an honest question, if there has been any honesty to go around. Pilate is baiting the crowd. He is playing by the rules that Rome has developed. He places himself squarely in the world of which Jesus' kingdom is not. He doesn't say, "Shall I crucify the son of God?" He changes the narrative. He presents Jesus as a king of a pathetic people. The shame is too great, so the people, who charged Jesus with blasphemy, become blasphemers in saying, "We have no king but Caesar." This is exactly what Pilate wants to hear. On the day of preparation for one of the holiest days of the year, the people have thrown away their God and recognized that the only power is Caesar. Pilate's job is secure, the people's sin is revealed, and Jesus is sent away to be crucified.

This seven-scene drama reveals one great lie that we like to tell ourselves: "There's nothing we can do." Pilate tries to present himself as innocent and that his hands are tied. "There's nothing we can do" is something that the powerful love to say when they don't agree with what the powerless need. There's always something we can do, though the students at St. Denis were quick to pick up arms and build barricades which will prove to be their undoing. Is there another way to bring about change without first picking up a musket?

Sam Wells tells a story about a large field that was next to a housing estate that had been fenced off by the county council.[2] Local residents had often asked to be able to use the field for sport and recreation, but there was always some excuse the council made to say that it was just not possible, mostly referring to the amount of debris on the field. So, one morning two parents arranged for the children of the neighborhood to clean up the field, and they invited the newspapers to record the event. They didn't tear down any fences, they didn't protest at the local civic hall. They simply dismantled the council's authority through good works. Interestingly, the council soon found the appropriate funds to purchase playground equipment.

They dismantled power through good. This is why we call Jesus' crucifixion "Good Friday." It reveals that truth and power rest in love, mercy, and great goodness. We are being called to offer a goodness within the world that death cannot swallow, a goodness that offers abundant life, a goodness that will outlast the powers and principalities that only know violence, oppression, and fear.

WE ALWAYS CHOOSE BARABBAS

All four Gospels record that the crowd was given a choice between Barabbas and Jesus, but in no other Gospel is the choice so telling as it is in Matthew's. Matthew's crafting of this choice reveals to us the very thin line between sin and righteousness. Sin is so tempting because sin is half-right. It misses the mark on God's first commandment—"be fruitful and multiply." Sin is great at multiplying, but it is never fruitful. Love of God and love of neighbor should always be our motivation as followers of Christ, and the way we share the core of our faith in the world is through multiplying fruitfulness. But sin is tempting because it is so close to being right. Like a cancer it multiplies with reckless abandon, but its multiplication only crowds out the good.

So the crowd is given a choice. In Matthew's Gospel, the choice is specifically between Jesus Barabbas and Jesus the Messiah. Barabbas means, "Son of the Father."[3] *Bar* means son. *Abba* means father, a term Jesus often uses for God. So the choice is between son of the father and son of the father. At first blush the choice is so close, maybe even difficult to distinguish, but the choice changes the trajectory of everything.

This choice reveals four different ways in which the Jewish people lived as an occupied people. Living into Jesus' passion necessitates understanding the power dynamic between occupier and the occupied. Jesus was crucified because he was a threat to those who were in power within both the religious elite and the Roman ruling class. Generally speaking there were four different Jewish groups living out their covenant with God in different ways. In part, the way they understood their relationship with God affected the way they understood how to live as an occupied people.

First there were the Sadducees, who were the keepers of the Temple. The most important thing was the Temple cult, making sacrifices, and keeping the hierarchical power in place. You can think of the Sadducees as the French upper class. Status held the highest importance. Therefore their relationship with Rome, or the monarchy in the case of *Les Misérables*, was one of collaboration. Rome allowed them to keep and maintain the Temple in Jerusalem. The military might of Rome helped maintain order in the land, and order is necessary in maintaining Temple practices. Though there is a great concession in recognizing that a sovereign Davidic kingdom was now a fantasy, and at worst, collaboration helped maintain a brutal oppression.

Next we have the Pharisees, who sought reformation. This reformation has deep roots in Jewish history. Much like the Babylonian Exile was seen as God's instrument of retribution for not following God's law, the Roman Empire was also a means of calling the people to "wake up," so to speak. So, much like Javert, the Pharisees had an obsession with following the Law. Order was a means of seeking righteousness. In following the Law, God would eventually overthrow Rome and establish David's kingdom once again. But keeping the Law to this degree was practically and economically impossible for most of the general public.

Then we have the Essenes, who decided to withdraw as a means of living under Roman rule. They did not seek to overthrow the government; rather they escaped from it for the sake of purifying the soul. Valjean plays the role of an Essene. For most of *Les Misérables* he is in hiding, hoping that his past will disappear with time. He's not just an escapist in that he doesn't enter the story, but he always wrestles with how much involvement he is called to offer. The Essenes took very seriously the importance of purity, welcoming the stranger, and keeping the Sabbath, but ignoring injustice in the world doesn't mean it goes away. They were very welcoming when you came, but rarely did they go out to find those who needed to know God's love.

Finally there are the Zealots—the restorationists. The Zealots had no problem with adopting armed resistance against the Roman government like Enjolras and the rest of the "Friends of the ABC." They weren't seeking to bring about a new kingdom, but to restore the golden age of Israel, so to speak. They weren't so concerned about the injustice of the Roman authority as much as they were concerned that it was Rome doing it. The problem is not that they were seeking too much, but too little—they wanted a personnel change, not a world in which the last shall be first.

Barabbas, being seen as a bandit and insurrectionist, would be identified with the Zealots. But in which category would Jesus be? Jesus' understanding of purity helps us understand how Jesus both shared things in common with these groups and yet was quite "other" against them. I would love to admit that we no longer have Sadducees, Pharisees, Essenes, and Zealots, that we no longer have people who would collaborate with a corrupt government as long as they could maintain their own sense of power and authority. I wish we no longer had Pharisees who are obsessed with everyone else's maintenance of discipline as opposed to their own, or that there were no longer people who simply withdraw thinking that if they create their own protective bubble from the world they can maintain purity, or people who use violence to perpetuate their own agenda.

Jesus held a high view of order but wasn't a Sadducee. Jesus said to the man healed of leprosy, "Go . . . and show yourself to the priest, and, as Moses commanded, make an offering for your cleansing, for a testimony to them" (Luke 5:14). But he also said, "Go and learn what this means, 'I desire mercy, not sacrifice'" (Matthew 9:13). Jesus was like the Pharisees in many ways but wasn't a Pharisee. Jesus spent most of his time teaching and redefining the law so that the law might be fulfilled. The redefining of the law often put him at odds with the Pharisees, such as when he says, It is not what goes into the body that defiles but what comes out.[4] Jesus touches the leper and allows the unclean to touch him. Jesus is also well aware that when he is crucified the Pharisees will see him as cursed according to Deuteronomy 21:23.

Jesus was like the Essenes and their love of purity, but Jesus wasn't an Essene. The Essenes felt they could not be pure without withdrawing and communing only with like-minded people. Jesus' words to love your enemy fly in the face of what is desperately close to escapism. Jesus also was all about revolution like the Zealots, but Jesus wasn't a Zealot. Jesus' call to put down the sword at his arrest is something completely foreign to those who would build barricades. Sam Wells says it well in *Power and Passion*, "Don't forget that Christianity is not so much about being clean as about being cleansed. Don't be so tough on yourself that you cannot see the glory of forgiveness and the gift God is giving you in this new relationship [in Christ]. The purity that matters most is your unambiguous willingness to accept the new life God is giving you in Jesus."[5]

This new life is not predicated upon hierarchy and order, as Jesus says that in the kingdom of God the last shall be first. This new life does not depend on keeping your hands ritually clean as much as it does on knowing when to get your hands dirty in order to be a "good" Samaritan. This new life does not depend on escaping the world but on redefining it. This new life is not about doing away with your enemy, but about loving your enemy and praying for those who persecute you.

The crowd chose Barabbas because they did not have a holy imagination to believe that Christ could change reality itself. Do we really believe in the power of Christ to upend our assumptions about the world? Do we really trust Christ enough to go learn what this means, "I desire mercy, not sacrifice"? Do we really recognize that God put on flesh and walked among us so that we would walk with each other rather than retreating into a protective bubble of our own creation? When given the choice, which "son of the father" will we choose?

TRAGEDY

Late in the evening the French National Guard attacks the barricades. The insurgents take shelter after bullets cut down several of their comrades. They manage to survive the night, and they fortify the barricade. Jean Valjean has joined the fight, and as day breaks, Enjolras has announced that a large infantry is approaching and no one is coming to their aid. With a hint of defeat, he sends those who have children away to return home. Soon after, there is a barrage of bullets, the National Guard breaks through their defenses after a brief stalemate, and almost all of the revolutionaries are slaughtered with only Valjean, Marius, and Javert escaping with their lives.

Seeing this scene portrayed on stage is certainly moving. At one moment the audience is filled with a revolutionary pride, and the next they experience a crushing defeat. Although I have never seen war with my own eyes, as a pastor I've heard stories of those who wrestle with what they've seen. I've heard that bullets don't care whether a man is good or bad. I've heard confessions of those who were ordered to take lives. I've heard of the stress from those who try to come home and live with their families as they once had, only to realize that part of them is still chained to their deployment.

I pray for a day that we realize that only Jesus' blood needed to be spilled. I think Jesus' first words from the cross, "Father, forgive them; for they do not know what they are doing" (Luke 23:34), are spoken over and over again when we build barricades, choose Barabbas, or think that revolution and resurrection are one and the same. Hearing Jesus say these words causes us to turn away in embarrassment. How can such grace be offered when we time and time again turn away from the Kingdom that Jesus began? How can the one who struggles to breathe on the cross use his final precious words to beg God to offer us forgiveness?

Interestingly Jesus doesn't say, "I forgive you." Throughout the Gospels, Jesus certainly expresses the authority to forgive:

> *"Which is easier, to say, 'Your sins are forgiven you,' or to say, 'Stand up and walk'? But so that you may know that the Son of Man has authority on earth to forgive sins"—he said to the one who was paralyzed—"I say to you, stand up and take your bed and go to your home." (Luke 5:23-24)*

In this case, Jesus can't. You can't forgive in the midst of tragedy. The suffering must subside before forgiveness can be offered. Forgiveness in the midst of violence suggests acceptance. The violence must subside, the sword must be put down, the bullets must stop flying before forgiveness can be offered. This is why Jesus, who has the authority to forgive, begs God, the Father, to show mercy on his murderers. There must be peace before there is forgiveness, and there must be forgiveness before there can be reconciliation.

When the barricades are built and bullets are fired, there is little turning back, and the only result is the continuation of humanity's violent story. Stanley Hauerwas writes, "Through the cross of Christ we are drawn into the mystery of the Trinity. This is God's work on our behalf. We are made members of a kingdom governed by a politics of forgiveness and redemption. The world is offered an alternative unimaginable by our sin-determined fantasies."[6]

In the musical, Marius returns to the scene where his friends would drink and discuss plans of revolution. He notices how the emptiness of the local pub reflects the emptiness and loss he is experiencing. There is guilt in his survival. There is regret that they seemed to have lost their lives for nothing. I've heard more than once in my conversations with veterans that, "It should have been me." I wonder if the disciples felt this kind of remorse, which is why they abandoned Jesus on the cross. Scripture suggests that their abandonment was rooted in fear, but maybe part of their fear is rooted in their own guilt for not being crucified with Jesus.

Marius sings that the barricade was their last communion with each other, and indeed it was. He struggles to make sense of what had happened. Don't we do the same? When we look at our own faults and failures, don't we question what we might have been thinking or why we thought this or that was a good idea? Jesus' begging for our forgiveness from God so often feels shamefully undeserved. The good news is the One who is our judge is also the One who loves us enough to die and rise again for us. The good news is that this story is not finished. Though the chairs might be empty with memories we hope to forget, Christ always remembers us. Christ's divine memory is not a cognizant exercise, but a "re-remembering" of our soul. Christ puts us back together in the places that have broken away. Even Marius, though broken and ashamed, yet has a role to play before the story's end. Thankfully, so do we.

6

THE BLESSED GARDEN: A HOPEFUL VISION

"Truly I tell you, today you will be with me in Paradise." (Luke 23:43)

This chapter is admittedly a departure from the rest of this book. Most of our story has focused on what happens in *Les Misérables*, how the characters reveal Christ, and why it matters. This chapter takes a slightly different approach. Much like poverty is an unnamed character in Hugo's story that unites all of the characters together, Hugo's use of gardens reveals another story just under the surface. When you hear the word *garden*, what comes to mind? Do you envision the hanging gardens of Babylon or tomatoes and peppers growing in a small plot of land? Is a garden a public green space for all to enjoy, or should it be locked away for personal use? Maybe you think of the garden of Eden, where God and humanity enjoy an unashamed communion? Maybe the garden of Gethsemane comes to mind, where Jesus agonized over God's will? Although it's hard to call the various gardens throughout *Les Misérables* a proper character in the story, they nevertheless carry Hugo's message from beginning to end.

THE TALE OF THREE GARDENS

The Bible is not a single book; rather it is a library of many books from many authors, editors, and sources. If the Bible were a single book, and I had the daunting task of assigning it a title, the most appropriate title would be "A Tale of Three Gardens." In the beginning God created a garden and placed humanity within it. Jesus' passion began in the garden of Gethsemane and ended with resurrection from a garden tomb. In the end there will be a river that waters the tree of life where God's radiance will shine forever. From Eden to Gethsemane to the new creation, gardens tell us almost everything we need to know about God, humanity, and God's love for humanity.

Creation is perplexing. We don't have to be here, and yet here we are. The universe would work perfectly without us, and this baffles both the scientist and the theologian alike. Theologians dive deep into the "why" of creation, but sometimes theologians are left scratching their heads about the "how" of creation. At least Scripture tells us that the universe was created in seven days, yet the earth looks billions of years old. Scientists have an answer for the "how" things came to be, but scientists are perplexed as to why anything exists at all. Some things exist for no apparent reason, like the mosquito, and other things we know exist, like the superposition of quantum particles; but they simply can't be observed. The universe doesn't have to be the way it is, but it is, and there's something mysteriously beautiful about this fact.

The same is true with the Creation account in Genesis. The first chapter of Genesis is full of beautiful, colorful, superfluous, ostentatious descriptions that don't need to be there, but they are. God names the light "Day," the darkness "Night," the heavens above "Sky," and the ground below "Earth." When God creates things, God doesn't leave them as things; God claims them and gives them a name. Not only does God give them a name, God provides purpose and a calling. The sun is in charge of the day, and the moon is in charge of the night. The waters and the earth below are charged with bringing forth life, the fish and the animals. God creates, names, and gives purpose. Let there be light so that there might be day, let there be water so that there might be fish, let there be humanity to till and keep the garden. The mystery of the universe, the "how" and the "why," can be found in everything. How—Let there be. Why—I love you. Let there be because I love you.

This first garden in God's story is God's word searching for a way to express itself. There's so much love bound up within the Godhead—the Father, Son, and Spirit—that it spills forth upon a formless void and God brings order to chaos. God's love is searching for a way to express itself, and waters part and mountains form. God's love is pouring out and plants sprout, fish swim, birds fly, animals creep, and humanity awakens. God's love is searching for a word to describe the unfathomable beauty of creation, and God says, "It is good, very good," and God and creation rest in each other. In essence, creation is love in search of a word.

The peace God and humanity shared in the garden of Eden was temporary. Originally humanity saw that God was good, a delight, and was to be desired; but the serpent, the most crafty of God's creations, led humanity to redirect our vision:

*When the woman saw that the **tree** was good for food, and that [**the tree**] was a delight to the eyes, and that the **tree** was to be desired to make one wise, she took of its fruit and ate; and she also gave some to her husband, who was with her, and he ate. Then the eyes of both were opened, and they knew that they were naked; and they sewed fig leaves together and made loincloths for themselves.*

(Genesis 3:6-7, emphasis added)

Humanity now viewed creation, and not the Creator, as the source of goodness, delight, and desire, so we could not stay within the garden. In an act of mercy, God fashioned clothes for the man and woman and sent them out to cultivate life from the ground up. Just as a seed sprouts within the darkness of the earth, and a child forms in the hidden sanctuary of a mother's womb, recognizing that God is indeed the one who cultivates growth would lead us to let go of idolizing creation and redirect our gaze to the heavens. It would have been too tempting to stay in the garden. Once humanity's eyes were "opened" to the shame of their own nakedness, simply tilling and keeping the garden would not be enough.

The second garden in our story is the work of God in the person of Jesus. John's Gospel introduces his story with, "In the beginning was the Word, and the Word was with God and the Word was God" (John 1:1). This Gospel wants us to remember that this story is a continuation of God's work from the beginning. Instead of fashioning clothes for humanity, God assumed humanity itself. God put on flesh and walked among us to show us what love looks like. Through teachings, healings, service, and glory, Christ was redirecting our gaze from our temptations of wealth, power, and influence, so that we might once again see God as the source of goodness, delight, and desire. On the last night Jesus was with his disciples, "he went out with his disciples across the Kidron valley to a place where there was a garden, which he and his disciples entered" (John 18:1). Although John's Gospel invites us to remember the details of Jesus' grief from the other Gospels, this garden is a place of suffering, anguish, and betrayal.

Jesus is led away from the garden of sorrow, but instead of receiving clothes he is stripped, beaten, and mocked. Instead of finding the tree of life, he is placed upon a tree of death. It's almost as if God set aside the tree of the knowledge of good and evil from the very beginning—"The LORD God commanded the man, 'You may freely eat of every tree of the garden; but of the tree of the knowledge of good and evil you shall not eat, for in the day that you eat of it you shall die'" (Genesis 2:16-17). It seems that God would later use this tree so that humanity might one day know the true difference between good and evil. But we wanted this knowledge on our own terms. So, God in the flesh of Jesus, was nailed to the cross, taking on the sin of humanity. And if we've missed the metaphor, Jesus tells the thief, "Truly I tell you, today you will be with me in paradise" (Luke 23:43 NIV), *paradise* meaning, "pleasure ground, orchard, garden"; the New Testament adds the meaning of "heaven."[1]

After breathing his last, Jesus is laid to rest in a garden tomb, and it seems that the story is over. On the third day, Mary comes to the tomb early in the morning to find that the stone already has been rolled away. Interestingly when she first sees the risen Lord, she mistakes him as the gardener. This is not a moment of mistaken identity; rather she sees Christ with the new eyes God came to establish through Christ. Gardening was God's first job, and now humanity can see the garden's source. Of course she thinks Christ is the gardener because he is! Our eyes now see that it is God, and not the tree, that is the source of goodness, delight, and desire.

The story isn't yet finished. At the end of it all, God will create a new heaven and a new earth. In this new place where heaven and earth are one and the same there will be *the river of the water of life, bright as crystal, flowing from the throne of God and of the Lamb through the middle of the street of the city. On either side of the river is the tree of life with its twelve kinds of fruit, producing its fruit each month; and the leaves of the tree are for the healing of the nations. Nothing accursed will be found there any more. But the throne of God and of the Lamb will be in it, and his servants will worship him; they will see his face, and his name will be on their foreheads. And there will be no more night; they need no light of lamp or sun, for the Lord God will be their light, and they will reign forever and ever.*

(Revelation 22:1-5)

It is both garden and city representing heaven and earth coming together, and in this holy place we will see the face of God. God will be the only source of light, and there we will rest in God's heart for eternity. From the garden of Eden to the garden of suffering and resurrection to the city garden where all things are one, God's story has always been about a garden and our place within it.

FINDING REST

Although Hugo isn't so explicit about God's story being that of three gardens, it seems that the gardens throughout *Les Misérables* are a symbol of God's presence. Early in the story we read that M. Bienvenu, the graceful priest who changes Valjean's life, walks through his garden every evening for a moment of Sabbath. The priest's great reverence of nature mirrors his great love of God. This evening spiritual discipline is probably why the priest is a constant source of grace and compassion in the community. In this case, the priest's garden represents Sabbath.

Daily spiritual practices help keep God's grace always before us. Every morning, at least when my children don't wake up at odd hours throughout the night, I keep the same prayer schedule. I go outside, spend some time simply breathing in and breathing out, and then I recite part of Psalm 51—"Create in me a clean heart, O God, / and put a new and right spirit within me. / Do not cast me away from your presence, / and do not take your holy spirit from me" (Psalm 51:10-11). Then I enter into prayer for friends, neighbors, and enemies, asking for God's presence to be made known to all. Before reciting the Lord's Prayer, I simply listen. Sometimes the silence is deafening. Sometimes the silence reveals what God is calling me to do.

> *On one occasion when Jesus was going to the house of a leader of the Pharisees to eat a meal on the sabbath, they were watching him closely. Just then, in front of him, there was a man who had dropsy. And Jesus asked the lawyers and Pharisees, "Is it lawful to cure people on the sabbath, or not?" But they were silent. So Jesus took him and healed him, and sent him away. Then he said to them, "If one of you has a child or an ox that has fallen into a well, will you not immediately pull it out on a sabbath day?" And they could not reply to this. (Luke 14:1-6)*

Silence can be deafening. Sometimes when I pray I can almost hear God's voice reminding me of my calling and showing me what I need to do. Other times . . . it's just silent. Jesus is invited to a Sabbath dinner party, and Scripture says that the religious leaders were watching him closely. Have you ever been on the other end of a "silent watching"? There are whispers between huddled people, and when you get too close the conversation stops? This story from Luke paints a vivid picture. Jesus is at dinner on the Sabbath, religious leaders are watching him closely from a distance, and then suddenly a man with dropsy appears. This man isn't an invited guest, or a friend of a friend who mistakenly joined the wrong party. This man is being used as a pawn of entrapment against Jesus.

Jesus, well aware of what was happening, asked the Pharisees, "Is it lawful to heal on the sabbath or not?" but they were silent. Were they silent because they did not know how to answer? Maybe they were silent because they wanted Jesus to answer his own question? Nevertheless, Jesus answers this silence with a healing. He heals the man and sends him away. Not only has Jesus healed him of a terrible disease, but by sending him away, he has also liberated this man from ever being the religious elite's pawn again.

Healing and liberation go hand in hand in the Gospels, and this is why the Pharisees never praise Jesus for the transformation and restoration he offers. During Jesus' lifetime, sickness and sin were indelibly linked. Illness was the result of sin, and therefore illness was deserved and often seen as a punishment. It's like when the disciples saw a blind man and asked, "Rabbi, who sinned, this man or his parents, that he was born blind?" (John 9:2). In a word, Jesus replied, "Neither." When Jesus healed the individual, he was also healing the community. When someone's health was restored, their place in the community was also restored. When the man who had dropsy was healed, there was no longer any reason for the Pharisees to keep him away from the synagogue. This brought about restoration of the community, but also chipped away at the religious elite's authority.

It is important that this healing happened on the Sabbath. Illness was thought of as a transgression. There certainly is a transgression in this story, but it is not at the hands of the man in need of healing. A transgression in the Hebrew Scriptures essentially means to pass through something without paying mind to it. Have you ever found yourself just going through the motions? Have you ever been distracted, and not paying attention to what you should? It's like at the end of the day when I'm scrolling through social media, and one of my children wants to read a book. I would be lying if I said I always immediately put my phone down.

In this story the Pharisees are "passing through without paying any mind." They are not mindful of the man they are using to entrap Jesus. They are not mindful that they have gathered on the Sabbath. They are not mindful of the deafening sound of their own silence when Jesus questions them. In this story, it is the religious elite, and not the man, who need forgiveness and healing for transgressions.

Sabbath is the antidote to transgression. Sabbath is a day of rest in which God is the only thing on our agenda. Sabbath is time set apart to be mindful of God and who God is calling us to be. In this way Sabbath is a silence that awakens our mind to the times when we have not been mindful. It is stunning how different my day is when I forget to keep my prayer schedule in the morning. When I forget to begin my day in prayer, I am often distracted, disgruntled, and stressed. "Set your minds on things that are above, not on things that are on earth" (Colossians 3:2). Setting our minds on God is the remedy to transgression.

M. Bienvenu's daily walks in his garden, surrounding himself with the beauty of God's creation, are a means of setting his mind on God. I don't mean to suggest that this generosity and grace are without sacrifice. Forgiving Valjean for stealing his silver and then gifting the rest of his silver to him after Valjean was caught by the police were certainly difficult decisions. But we can see that in this moment the priest's mind was "set on things that are above." It almost seems to come naturally to him. The more often we take Sabbath rest, the more often we take time to wander and meander with God, the more we become who God intends us to be. In this moment, M. Bienvenu knows that Valjean's soul is more precious than any silver he could ever possess. He is mindful of things that are above, and his Sabbath mindfulness is what sets the entirety of *Les Misérables* in motion.

A GARDEN'S DIFFICULT WORK

I am a bit envious of the man and the woman who were placed in the garden of Eden. The garden was already there, containing everything that they would ever need. Their job was to till it and keep it going. I do not have a green thumb. I have tried to grow vegetables and flowers in our backyard, but it always ends with dead, brown twigs and dry soil. Maybe if I woke up one morning to a garden already ready for harvesting I might have a better shot at keeping things alive. When friends come over to the house and see our pots of dry soil in the backyard, I jokingly tell them that it is an artwork installation titled "Potential." This rarely gets a laugh.

Gardens are a place for Sabbath rest, but they also take a great deal of work. When Valjean and a young Cosette are running for their lives from Javert's pursuit not long after they first enter Paris, Valjean seeks refuge in a convent garden. He calls out to the gardener hoping that he might show him grace. The gardener happens to be Fauchelevent, the man whom Valjean saved from being crushed by a horse cart back in Montreuil. Hope is never far from a garden, and Valjean's kindness is being repaid at a most convenient time. Fauchelevent takes them in, helps them escape, and aids them in finding semi-permanent residence in the convent itself. In exchange for the convent offering them lodging, and taking Cosette as a student, Valjean agrees to be the assistant gardener. Valjean finally finds respite, and it is no accident that this peace comes from his work as a gardener.

Gardening is hard work, so I hear. The Lord tells Moses in Leviticus 25:1-5 that the people can work the land for six years, but in the seventh year the land should rest.

The LORD spoke to Moses on Mount Sinai, saying: Speak to the people of Israel and say to them: When you enter the land that I am giving you, the land shall observe a sabbath for the LORD. Six years you shall sow your field, and six years you shall prune your vineyard, and gather in their yield; but in the seventh year there shall be a sabbath of complete rest for the land, a sabbath for the LORD: you shall not sow your field or prune your vineyard. You shall not reap the aftergrowth of your harvest or gather the grapes of your unpruned vine: it shall be a year of complete rest for the land.

Six years they can sow and prune, but in the seventh year they are to let the land yield what it will. There's something beautiful about the language of sowing and pruning. It's the two bookends that have to happen before the harvest. Sowing means that the ground has been overturned, the type of crop decided, and the boundaries marked. It's like when you begin a new ministry. Has your community of faith ever embarked on a new ministry? It's difficult work to map out how you will answer God's call through planning, preparing, recruiting, and implementation. Without taking the time to sow a specific seed, overturn the soil, and organize the garden, it will be difficult to reap any kind of fruitful harvest.

The other side of sowing is pruning. I love how the text doesn't say that you plant the seeds and God makes all of your crops grow perfectly with no need of cultivation or trimming or uprooting. Some folks think that when we begin a relationship with Christ, suddenly we have no problems. It's like when you leave the baptismal font, all of a sudden your spouse is beautiful, your kids are smart, your bank account is full, and your house appreciates. Unfortunately this isn't so. There is a pruning that happens. Being in Christ means we now know that we have to let go of the idols we've made, whether they damage our own body, our relationships, or our holy connection with God. God is saying that when the people enter into the Promised Land they are to spend six years cultivating the land, not only the earth, but also their connection to it. Imagine if when you join the church, the community asks that you spend six years planting seeds and pruning what needs to be thrown away before becoming a full member in your seventh year.

God also goes on to say that the land should rest. In the seventh year they are not to sow or prune, but to let the land be. They can eat what the land produced, but the land was to produce the harvest on its own. This is to remind the people that God is the source of life and abundance. Sometimes when we do a great job of sowing and pruning, we forget that it is God who offers growth. Letting the land rest reminded the people that the land was a gift. They didn't own it. God offered it to them.

After seven Sabbath years, the Jewish community is called together to join in what's called "The Jubilee." The Jubilee is a time in which debts are forgiven and land returns to its ancestral owner. Valjean is desperately seeking this kind of reset, but before he can find peace, he is resigned to continue planting, pruning, and cultivating. He does find peace knowing that Cosette is cared for, and Javert is none the wiser in where he is. Have you ever desired a Jubilee? Have you ever wanted a divine "reset button" on your life?

When I was in the fourth or fifth grade, I remember playing a Nintendo game, *Rampage*, all day. This was in a time when there was no "Save" feature in video games. If you wanted to play the game until the end, most of the time you just had to sit and play it. I was playing *Rampage*, a game where you are a monster and you destroy as much as you can on three different levels per state of the union. I remember being on Hawaii, the last level, when my youngest sister came into the room to tell me that supper was ready. I told her that I would be finished in just a few minutes. I was so close to beating the game. She momentarily left the room but came back with more fervor and authority. We went back and forth for a moment, and instead of hearing my cry that the game would soon be finished, she walked up to the console and pressed the Reset button. Thankfully I was so shocked at what she had done that I didn't have the presence of mind to punch her dead in the face, and she ran out of the room too fast for me to get her anyway.

I wish pressing the Reset button on our past was this easy. It isn't. Forgiveness and reconciliation are difficult work. It's no accident why God's time frame for the Jubilee is once every fifty years. Sometimes it seems that forgiveness takes just as long. Peter asks how often he should forgive his brother. Seven times? Jesus replies, More like seventy times seven times.

Cultivating a garden takes great work, and so does forgiveness. What might my home garden look like if I invest six years of sowing and pruning into it? What might my relationships look like if I worked for six years in intentional community building? I would imagine that resting in the peace of all our hard work would be more fruitful than we could ever imagine. The garden in which Valjean finds himself is a reminder of the hard work that lies ahead, but it is also a symbol of peace and rest from his past. It is a symbol of the Jubilee he hopes he will one day find.

CULTIVATION OF THE WILD

Not all gardens are ordered, pruned, and manicured. Sometimes a garden's beauty rests in letting it naturally grow. Think about a nature preserve or national forest. The difficult work in this case is keeping the outside world at bay. Rue Plumet, Valjean's home later in the story, has a garden, but it is unruly and wild. This garden is where Cosette and Marius choose to meet and profess their love for each other. The garden represents the wild and passionate desire that they have for each other, as well as their longing to keep their relationship a secret from the outside world.

Sometimes when we try to make sense of the world around us, it's like putting together a puzzle when we don't quite have all of the pieces. It's like when Jesus asked the disciples, "Who do people say that I am?" Some said that Jesus was a prophet. Some said he was Elijah. Some said that he was John the Baptist back from the dead. It's not that they were wrong, but their picture of Jesus was limited. Jesus certainly was a prophet. He was a healer like Elijah. He did speak a difficult truth like John the Baptist, and yet he was more. Jesus then asked the disciples, "Who do you say that I am?" Peter confessed, "You are the Messiah." Peter spoke the truth, though Peter didn't understand the truth he had spoken.

Hugo's gardens serve as diversely beautiful backdrops reflecting characters' grounding in their relationships or the world around them. For the priest the garden represents Sabbath. For Valjean a garden is hard work. For Cosette and Marius it is wild and passionate. What is our relationship with God's creation?[2] Sometimes our relationship with creation is like the man and woman in the garden of Eden. From this perspective, nature is something unspoiled and idyllic. Nature reminds us of whence we came and where we're going. Henry David Thoreau said, "We need the tonic of wildness. . . . We require that all things be mysterious and unexplorable, that land and sea be indefinitely wild, unsurveyed and unfathomed by us because [it is] unfathomable. We can never have enough of Nature"[3] The good of this perspective is that it recognizes nature's beauty, but it fails to see that we have to work the land and irrigate fields; nor does it recognize the circle of life, so to speak.

We might also look at nature through a scientific lens. I don't know whether it's humbling or baffling or awe-inspiring, but almost everything we observe in nature can be expressed as a mathematical formula. Think of a video game or a flight simulator. Almost everything can be expressed in binary code—0 and 1. It is mind-boggling to think about just how far down the rabbit hole this goes in terms of what is real and what is not, but this view seems to miss something.

I'm not saying that E=Mc² isn't elegant, but a flower seems to be more beautiful. For example, in 2013 the Intergovernmental Panel on Climate Change made a report that claimed:

> The globally averaged combined land and ocean surface temperature data as calculated by a linear trend, show a warming of 0.85 [0.65 to 1.06] °C, over the period 1880–2012, when multiple independently produced datasets exist. . . . The total increase between the average of the 1850–1900 period and the 2003–2012 period is 0.78 [0.72 to 0.85] °C . . . based on the single longest dataset available.[4]

I applaud the precision, but in this case maybe a picture is worth a thousand words.

Sometimes looking at nature can stir up something inside of us, an anger at the way that humanity hasn't kept the garden as we should. It is important to know that in the short time humanity has been on the planet, we've very quickly done a lot of damage; but sometimes anger on one side is only met with anger from another. There is certainly a time to be filled with a righteous and holy anger, but when we start to speak at each other instead of with each other, our anger, on both sides, becomes an idol that we have a difficult time tearing down, even when our "side" has won. It is interesting to note that when the barricades are built and the people are at war with one another, all of the public gardens are closed.

Nature can also be seen as an economy. A strawberry is beautiful. It's arguably even more beautiful when you can sell it at the market so we can enjoy it in our ice cream. For example, research has shown that the Clean Air Act signed into law in 2010 has "prevented thirteen million lost workdays, improving worker productivity which contributes to a stronger economy . . . [and] kept kids healthy and in school, avoiding 3.2 million lost school days due to respiratory illness and other diseases caused or exacerbated by air pollution." The summary of the research on the economic impacts of the act noted that cleaner air improved crop and timber yields, and that by 2020 the act will have created economic benefits outweighing its costs by a ratio of thirty to one.[5] Our environment and our economy go hand in hand, and clean air is a good thing. Of course, there are multiple strategies of how to keep air clean while also maintaining a robust economy. Gardens aren't always works of art, but are a way of life. Valjean wasn't tending the garden in the convent for the sake of making something beautiful. It was the way he supported himself.

Sometimes nature can be out of sight, and out of mind. We aren't connected to the environment as we once were as a culture, which makes it difficult to understand and appreciate the role nature plays in our daily life. For example, as late as 1870, almost fifty percent of the US working population was employed in agriculture.[6] By 2008, that figure had dropped to less than two percent.[7] It's hard to miss how often Hugo wants us to stop and relish the beauty and importance of nature. Although in the musical, Marius and Cosette's meeting is the only time a garden is on stage, it certainly plays a central role in the story Hugo is trying to tell. Marius and Cosette's love for each other is wild, passionate, and spontaneous, so the garden in which they find themselves is the same. Have you considered how your view of nature reflects your perspective of other things? Is nature a luxury that is opposite to your everyday experience? Is the cultivation of nature your way of life? Is our treatment of nature a point of antagonism, or maybe it hasn't crossed your mind how the strawberries get to the market.

GOD IS STILL AT WORK

At the end of it all, Hugo means to show that the gardens throughout *Les Misérables* represent the different aspects of grace.

Sometimes grace offers peace. Sometimes offering grace takes great work. Sometimes grace is wild and unexpected. It's beautiful to ponder for a moment that we are always surrounded by God's symphony of nature. Every time we draw a breath we should give thanks for the grace God has offered to us. God's loving presence is all around us if we have eyes to see it.

I think Colossians 1:15-20 expresses this well.

He is the image of the invisible God, the firstborn of all creation; for in him all things in heaven and on earth were created, things visible and invisible, whether thrones or dominions or rulers or powers—all things have been created through him and for him. He himself is before all things, and in him all things hold together. He is the head of the body, the church; he is the beginning, the firstborn from the dead, so that he might come to have first place in everything. For in him all the fullness of God was pleased to dwell, and through him God was pleased to reconcile to himself all things, whether on earth or in heaven, by making peace through the blood of his cross.

These verses are a hymn telling the story of who Christ is and how Christ is the glue of all creation. Have you ever wondered what God looks like? I love asking children to draw a picture of what they think God looks like. As a child we typically draw God as an old man with a large beard sitting on a throne somewhere in the clouds. Later, as we grow older, our picture of God changes. Sometimes we see God as small and intimate, symbolized with a heart or hands holding. Sometimes we picture God as larger than we can imagine, full of majesty and glory, holding all things together in infinite wisdom, justice, and love. How would you answer the question, "What does God look like?" The good news is we don't have to guess. This Christ hymn from Colossians begins by saying, Christ "is the image of the invisible God, the firstborn of all creation." God looks like the work of Jesus—speaking truth to power, healing the sick, feeding the hungry, challenging the disciples, and loving the outcast. Christ is also the firstborn of all creation, which means Christ is where we begin, and where it all began.

I love noting that the word *perfect* isn't in either Genesis creation account. When God was creating the heavens and the earth, God said that it was good, which means that there was room for the growth of the grace of Jesus Christ from the very beginning. The Gospel of John puts it, "All things came into being through him, and without him not one thing came into being" (John 1:3). The Colossian hymn says the same: "In him all things in heaven and on earth were created, things visible and invisible, whether thrones or dominions or rulers or powers—all things have been created through him and for him" (Colossians 1:16). In other words, Jesus is where we begin.

Christ isn't just where we begin with our relationship with God; rather it is where we are and where we should always find ourselves. "In him all the fullness of God was pleased to dwell" (Colossians 1:19). Jesus is the incarnation of God, or "God in the flesh." There are two words in the New Testament that mean flesh—*anthropos* and *sarx*. *Anthropos* is a more simple term suggesting humanity or what we might say as "flesh and blood." When Scripture says "the Word became flesh," *sarx* is used, which means that what Christ assumed wasn't just humanity, but creation itself. Part of being a Christian is to see that we are intimately connected to the world around us. Christ, through whom all things came into being, is also the presence of God that holds all things together through grace.

Christ is where we begin, Christ is where we are, and Christ is where we will be.

I saw no temple in the city, for its temple is the Lord God the Almighty and the Lamb. And the city has no need of sun or moon to shine on it, for the glory of God is its light, and its lamp is the Lamb. The nations will walk by its light, and the kings of the earth will bring their glory into it. Its gates will never be shut by day—and there will be no night there. (Revelation 21:22-25).

When the new heaven and the new earth become one, when God brings God's story to a close, Christ, the Lamb of God, is there offering perpetual light on all the good work that God has done. There at the end of it all, all of God's creation will come together at the foot of the tree of life for the "healing of the nations" (Revelation 22:2).

Until then there is still work to be done. During the uprising of 1832, when all of the public gardens are closed, Hugo mentions that there are two children who snuck into the garden to find food. It seems that being at war with each other causes us to forget the least of us. At the end of the story, when everything seems right in the world of our main characters, Hugo mentions the two children again. It seems that they have been forgotten. They are still begging for food. They are still looking for shelter. They have no garden for Sabbath, to work, or to love. It is a reminder to us all that our work is never done. Maybe this is the true grace of *Les Misérables*. Hugo takes us on a journey through the need for redemption, the importance of justice, the sin of poverty, the joy of love, the sacrifice of revolution, and the beauty of God's presence. And then, at the end, there is a graceful reminder that there is still work to be done for the glory of God. Thankfully Lent is a gift, offering us time to wrestle, discern, and practice the ways we might continue God's graceful work.

Acknowledgments

Thank you so much to the Abingdon Team for making this project possible, especially Susan, Lauren, Tim, Maria, Chuck, and Angie. Thank you to my wife who still loves me even when I'm knee-deep in a project. A special thank you to Conductor Evan Roider whose backstage tour of the *Les Misérables* National Tour stage was just the inspiration I needed. I pray that this work will be a blessing to all who read!

NOTES

CHAPTER 1.
GRACE WELL RECEIVED: THE STORY OF JEAN VALJEAN

1. Victor Hugo, *Les Misérables*, trans. Norman Denny (Penguin Books: London, 1976), 111.
2. Hugo, *Les Misérables*, 64.
3. Paraphrased from Gil Rendle's book *Doing the Math of Mission: Fruits, Faithfulness, and Metrics* (Lanham, MD: The Rowman & Littlefield Publishing Group, Inc., 2014), 51.
4. James C. Howell, *The Will of God: Answering the Hard Questions* (Louisville, KY: Westminster John Knox Press, 2009), 22.
5. John Wesley, "Wesley's Four Resolutions," from chapter 2 in *The Journal of John Wesley*, ed. Percy Livingstone Parker (Chicago: Moody Press, 1951), Christian Classics Ethereal Library (CCEL), https://www.ccel.org/ccel/wesley/journal.vi.ii.xi.html, accessed September 19, 2019.

CHAPTER 2.
WHEN GRACE AND JUSTICE COLLIDE: THE STORY OF JAVERT

1. Hugo, *Les Misérables*, 1107.
2. Augustine of Hippo, *Confessions*, trans. Maria Boulding (New York: Vintage Books, 1998), 30.
3. Dietrich Bonhoeffer, *Ethics*, trans. Reinhard Krauss and Charles C.

West (Minneapolis: Fortress Press, 2015), 197.

4. Samuel Wells, "It's the Economy, Stupid: A Sermon Preached in Duke University Chapel for Baccalaureate 2006 by the Revd Canon Dr Sam Wells," https://chapel-archives.oit.duke.edu/documents/sermons/2006/060513.pdf, accessed September 7, 2019.

CHAPTER 3.
THE POOR ARE ALWAYS WITH YOU: THE STORY OF FANTINE

1. Hugo, *Les Misérables*, 620.
2. "Go to Dark Gethsemane," by James Montgomery, *The United Methodist Hymnal* (Nashville: The United Methodist Publishing House, 1989), 290, stanza 3.
3. "Epilogue," final song in *Les Misérables* the musical; original French lyrics by Alain Boublil and Jean-Marc Natel; English-language libretto by Herbert Kretzmer.
4. "Grace Greater than Our Sin," Julia H. Johnston; hymn first appeared in *Hymns Tried and True*; Daniel B. Towner, composer and editor, 1911; *The United Methodist Hymnal*, 365.
5. Samuel Wells, *Improvisation: The Drama of Christian Ethics* (Grand Rapids, MI: Brazos Press, 2004), 149.

CHAPTER 4.
THE GIFT OF LOVE: THE STORY OF MARIUS AND COSETTE

1. Hugo, *Les Misérables*, 1118.
2. Matt Miofsky and Jason Byassee, *Eight Virtues of Rapidly Growing Churches* (Nashville: Abingdon Press, 2018), 2.
3. Ken Evers-Hood, *The Irrational Jesus: Leading the Fully Human Church* (Eugene, OR: Cascade Books, 2016), 9.
4. Hugo, *Les Misérables*, 538.
5. Matthew Richard Schlimm, *70 Hebrew Words Every Christian Should Know* (Nashville: Abingdon Press, 2018), 123.
6. Søren Kierkegaard, "Works of Love," *The Essential Kierkegaard*, ed. and trans. Howard V. Hong and Edna H. Hong (Princeton, NJ: Princeton University Press, 1997), 294.

CHAPTER 5.
BUILDING THE BARRICADE: THE STORY OF *LES AMIS*

1. Hugo, *Les Misérables*, 555.
2. Samuel Wells, *Power and Passion: Six Characters in Search of*

Resurrection (Grand Rapids, MI: Zondervan, 2007), 49.

3. See note in the Revised Standard Version of the Bible at Matthew 27:16: "Other ancient authorities read *Jesus Barabbas.*"

4. See Matthew 15:11.

5. Wells, *Power and Passion*, 77.

6. Stanley Hauerwas, *Cross-Shattered Christ: Meditations on the Seven Last Words* (Grand Rapids, MI: Brazos Press, 2004), 31.

Chapter 6.
The Blessed Garden: A Hopeful Vision

1. "Paradise," *The New Westminster Dictionary of the Bible*, ed. Henry Snyder Gehman (Philadelphia: The Westminster Press, 1970), 702.

2. *Green Faith: Mobilizing God's People to Save the Earth*, by Fletcher Harper (Nashville: Abingdon Press, 2015), is a great resource in answering this question.

3. Henry David Thoreau, chapter "Spring," in *Walden; or, Life in the Woods*, The Project Gutenberg EBook of Walden, last updated October 20, 2018, http://www.gutenberg.org/files/205/205-h/205-h.htm, accessed September 18, 2019.

4. Intergovernmental Panel on Climate Change, "152.4.3 Global Combined Land and Sea Surface Temperature," IPCC Wiki, https://ipcc.fandom.com/wiki/152.4.3_Global_Combined_Land_and_Sea_Surface_Temperature, accessed September 19, 2019.

5. "Clean Air Act Overview: The Clean Air Act and the Economy," United States Environmental Protection Agency, https://www.epa.gov/clean-air-act-overview/clean-air-act-and-economy, accessed September 19, 2019.

6. Patricia A. Daly, "Agricultural Employment: Has the Decline Ended?" in *Monthly Labor Review* from the U.S. Department of Labor Bureau of Labor Statistics, November 1981, 12, https://www.bls.gov/opub/mlr/1981/11/art2full.pdf, accessed September 23, 2019.

7. "Employment Projections: Employment by Major Industry Sector," U.S. Department of Labor Bureau of Labor Statistics, last modified September 4, 2019, https://www.bls.gov/emp/tables/employment-by-major-industry-sector.htm, accessed September 23, 2019.

The Grace of *Les Misérables*

The Grace of Les Misérables
978-1-5018-8710-9
978-1-5018-8711-6 eBook

The Grace of Les Misérables / DVD
978-1-5018-8714-7

The Grace of Les Misérables / Leader Guide
978-1-5018-8712-3
978-1-5018-8713-0 eBook

The Grace of Les Misérables / Youth Study Book
978-1-5018-8721-5
978-1-5018-8722-2 eBook

The Grace of Les Misérables / Worship Resources
978-1-5018-8723-9 Flash Drive
978-1-5018-8724-6 Download

The Grace of Les Misérables / Leader Kit
978-1-5018-8725-3

Also by Matt Rawle
The Gift of the Nutcracker
The Faith of a Mockingbird
Hollywood Jesus
The Salvation of Doctor Who
The Redemption of Scrooge
What Makes a Hero?

with Magrey R. deVega, Ingrid McIntyre, and April Casperson
Almost Christmas: A Wesleyan Advent Experience

with Juan Huertas and Katie McKay-Simpson
The Marks of Hope: Where the Spirit Is Moving in a Wounded Church

Made in the USA
Monee, IL
28 December 2023

50628137R00081